Sermons For Lent/Easter Based On Gospel Texts For Cycle C

Taking The Risk Out Of Dying

Lee Griess

CSS Publishing Company, Inc., Lima, Ohio

SERMONS FOR LENT/EASTER BASED ON GOSPEL TEXTS FOR CYCLE C:
TAKING THE RISK OUT OF DYING

Copyright © 1997 by
CSS Publishing Company, Inc.
Lima, Ohio

Some scripture quotations are from the *Holy Bible, New International Version.* Copyright 1973, 1978, 1984 International Bible Society. Used by permission of Zondervan
Bible Publishers. All rights reserved.

Some scripture quotations are from the *Revised Standard Version of the Bible,* copy-
righted 1946, 1952 ©, 1971, 1973, by the Division Education of the National Council of
the Churches of Christ in the USA. Used by permission.

Some scripture quotations are taken from *The Living Bible* © 1971. Used by permission
of Tyndale House Publishers, Inc., Wheaton IL 60189. All rights reserved.

Library of Congress Cataloging-in-Publication Data

Griess, Lee, 1950-
    Sermons for Lent/Easter based on Gospel texts for cycle C : taking the risk out of
dying / Lee Griess.
        p.   cm.
    ISBN 0-7880-1030-1 (pbk.)
    1. Lenten sermons. 2. Eastertide—Sermons. 3. Bible. N.T. Gospels—Sermons. 4.
Sermons, american. I. Title.
BV4277.G75   1997
252'.62—dc21

96-53601
CIP

This book is available in the following formats, listed by ISBN:
    0-7880-1030-1   Book
    0-7880-1031-X   MAC
    0-7880-1032-8   IBM 3 1/2
    0-7880-1093-X   Sermon Prep

PRINTED IN U.S.A.

Dedication:

to those I love —
especially my two kids, Krista and Ty,
who have endured their dad's preaching,
mostly from the pulpit,
with patience and good humor.
I hope some is remembered!

Editor's Note Regarding The Lectionary

During the past two decades there has been an attempt to move in the direction of a uniform lectionary among various Protestant denominations.

Preaching on the same scripture lessons every Sunday is a step in the right direction of uniting Christians of many faiths. If we are reading the same scriptures together, we may also begin to accomplish other achievements. Our efforts will be strengthened through our unity.

Beginning with Advent 1995 The Evangelical Lutheran Church in America dropped its own lectionary schedule and adopted the Revised Common Lectionary.

Reflecting this change, resources published by CSS Publishing Company put their major emphasis on the Revised Common Lectionary texts for the church year.

Table Of Contents

Introduction

A drum roll sounds and the cavernous Big Top goes dark. Suddenly, silhouetted in the circle of light, a single tightrope walker steps out into the light. His is the solitary task of making the walk from one end of the high wire to the other.

Such is the task of the preacher. Every Sunday morning countless Christian congregations gather for worship around liturgy, singing, and sermon — often giving the sermon the largest allotted period of time. How will I begin? What will I say? How can I be sure the words I speak have meaning to the congregation? Surely, these and other questions fill the minds of preachers each week. Not unlike the tightrope walker, each preacher wonders how to make it safely across the gap.

I share these sermons with the reader in the hope that they will touch the hearts of those who read them, share some illustrations with others engaged in the task of preaching, and perhaps give insight into the task of preaching that I so enjoy.

As you read these sermons, please note the use of the pronouns — they are usually in the third person and intentionally so. For the sermons, first and foremost, represent preaching to myself. As I struggle with the text, search for illustration, and finally put Word into proclamation, the first principle I use is to ask myself how the sermon can speak to me. What is God's Word saying to me today? How is God attempting to touch my life? What is God urging me to be, to do, to say to others? If I can adequately answer these questions, then I will have made it safely to the other side.

Secondly, pronouns are important because they give the listener a clue as to where the preacher walks. I have found that when the sermon uses too many second person pronouns, my preaching becomes too directed *at* the listener, rather than inviting the listener to include him or herself along with me under God's Word of grace or judgment. Don't get me wrong. There are times when second person pronouns must be used. At times preaching must also be prophetic and the preacher must be proclamatory, speaking God's Word *to* others. But for the most part, I have found that preaching must be inclusive — not only by use of gender sensitive language, but also in proclamation, including the listener and preacher together in sermon.

Finally, as you read the sermons, you will find them filled with illustrations. That is very important to me. A well-placed illustration can do more to help the preacher and listener come together under God's Word than a whole sheet of text. It is through the illustration that the point the preacher wishes to make comes to life and speaks the truth in its own words. I remember a cartoon that appeared in *Leadership* magazine a while back. It showed a couple of Pharisees on the edge of the crowd listening to Jesus. One remarked to the other regarding Jesus, "In my opinion, he needs to use fewer parables and more scripture!" Jesus knew what he was doing — inviting the listener to actively engage with him as the listener identified with the illustration and allowed the illustration to teach the truth Jesus spoke. We can learn something from the way Jesus chose to make His point. Sermons must be illustrative. It is there that the listener and preacher join in sharing the truth.

I hope the collection of sermons can be informative, instructive, and illustrative to those who read them. My thanks to the congregations who have served as mentors to me in the process of discovering God's Word and learning to be more effective in sharing it through my preaching. God bless.

— Lee Griess

The Mark
Upon Us

Ash Wednesday   *Matthew 6:1-6, 16-21*

One of the most striking television movies made in the last
few years was one called *Helter Skelter*. It was the story of the
cult worship and murder spree by the Charles Manson family in
California nearly three decades ago. In the closing moments of
the movie, Charles Manson and the members of his so-called family
are shown on the screen with their heads shaved and big "X" marks
on their foreheads. The stark appearance of the members of that
group which called itself a "family" and the "X" marks on their
foreheads were a visual, gruesome reminder of their involvement
in murder and death. The producers of that movie, I am sure,
intended just that image — the "X" to stand as a symbol of the
terrible acts those persons committed.

That "X" stands opposite Jesus' words in the Gospel reading
— that we allow no mark of our piety to separate us from those
around us, that our faith not be a visible kind of mark we wear on
our foreheads, but rather that it be the deep, heartfelt expression of
our love of God that is visible in the lives we live, not the acts of
piety that we perform for others to see.

I can't help but think of that "X" however, and its stark reminder
that there is another mark that we all bear upon us, not only the
mark of false piety, of religion done for show, but the deeper, more
scarring mark of sin that is also part of all of our lives. In spite of

9

Jesus' call for works of kindness done for their own reward and prayer done in secret, there is a need for us to begin Lent by looking deeper. And that is, in fact, the thrust of the reading from Matthew this evening. Jesus' words tell us to look within and to see the mark upon each of us.

Beginning with the first pages of the Bible and the story of Adam and Eve, the Bible pulls no punches. In the picture of that first man and woman and their rebellion toward God, we see ourselves echoed in this portrayal of humanity. Adam and Eve turn their back on God and are marked with death. Cain slays his brother, Abel, and he, too, is marked. In fact, throughout the Scriptures, there is an image, a picture of humanity, that is reflected even in our world today. It is a picture of willful rebellion against God, sinful disobedience, a desire to do our own thing, to use religion as a show, to parade our goodness in front of others and, in doing so, hide the mark of sin upon us. What we forget, however, is that no matter how proudly we parade our own goodness, God sees within. And when God looks upon us, the mark remains, as surely as if a big "X" were stamped on our foreheads.

It's unpleasant to think of these things. And I'm sure we'd rather not be reminded of them. Nevertheless, we are marked by death, each of us, just as certain as if we were part of that Manson family, or had participated with Adam and Eve in eating the fruit, or had joined with Cain in taking his brother's life. We are marked by death. And even though we cannot see it, a big "X" remains on our foreheads.

Today we begin our journey of Lent, these forty days of preparation. It is a path that leads to the cross and we begin it appropriately enough on Ash Wednesday. On this day many churches observe the tradition of distributing ashes on the foreheads of the worshipers. It's an ancient practice, reflecting the traditions of the Old Testament where people put on sackcloth and used ashes as an outward sign of repentance. The ashes were to remind them of their inward and heartfelt sorrow and repentance for the sin that could only lead to separation from God and death. And ashes can be a symbol for us as well, not only of our sorrow and repentance, but also of the certain mark of death that we each bear upon our foreheads.

The sobering thought is, however, that whether we bear the ashes on our foreheads or not, we are all marked; we all carry the sign of our sinful condition. The Bible tells us, "All have sinned and fallen short of the glory of God." And "the wages of sin is death." As Adam and Eve are driven from the Garden, God makes it clear when God says, "Dust you are and to dust you shall return." Those same words echo each time we stand at a grave in the cemetery when the Scripture is read which says, "Ashes to ashes, dust to dust."

Sobering, indeed, if that were it — an indelible mark that we all must carry. But that is not the extent of it. For as Christians we all bear another mark as well, another word has been spoken of us, another promise made. For over the mark of death is etched the sign of the cross, over top the "X" of our sinfulness is placed the gift of forgiveness. For we children of God bear another mark that distinguishes us as clearly as the big "X" mark labeled the Manson family, and it is the mark of baptism. In the Sacrament of Baptism we receive God's washing of forgiveness. The black mark of death is washed from our foreheads, the "X" of our sinfulness removed.

Sin and the power of Satan, the shackles of evil and death, no longer have claim on our lives. We are set free and another mark is laid upon us. The prophet Isaiah speaks of this very mark when he says, "Surely he took up our infirmities and carried our sorrows, yet we considered him stricken by God, smitten and afflicted. But he was pierced for our transgressions, he was crushed for our iniquities; the punishment that brought us peace was upon him, and by his wounds we are healed."

Through baptism we are linked for all time to Christ. Our baptism unites us in the death and resurrection of Jesus. Through our baptism we are claimed by God and made part of GOD'S family. In baptism we receive our name and are marked with God's grace forever. Perhaps you haven't noticed but during the Service of Holy Baptism the pastor says the person's name and continues saying, "Child of God, you have been sealed by the Holy Spirit and marked with the cross of Christ forever." And as the pastor says that, the pastor traces the mark of a cross on the person's forehead.

It is a moment of grace. The canceling of one sign and the receiving of another. And it happens each time we gather in worship, each time we offer ourselves in service to others, each time we close ourselves off in prayer, and each time we offer ourselves to God.

We begin the Lenten journey this year by recognizing the marks upon us, by reaffirming the lasting mark of grace that is ours through Holy Baptism, and by dedicating ourselves to be a mark of God's love in the lives of others — not by parading our goodness before others, but by allowing our lives, in their coming and going, to be the mark of God's grace. Amen.

Overcoming
Temptation

                                              Luke 4:1-13

This morning's Gospel reading sets the theme for us today, an appropriate theme as we begin our observance of Lent — the theme of sin and temptation. It's an appropriate one because it is one with which we all struggle.

I recently read a story about a little boy named Bobby who desperately wanted a new bicycle. His plan was to save his nickels, dimes and quarters until he finally had enough to buy a new 10-speed. Each night he asked God to help him save his money. Kneeling beside his bed, he prayed, "Dear Lord, please help me save my money for a new bike, and please, Lord, don't let the ice cream man come down the street again tomorrow."

Jim Grant in *Reader's Digest* a few months back told about an overweight businessman who decided it was time to shed some excess pounds. He took his new diet seriously, even changing his driving route to avoid his favorite bakery. One morning, however, he showed up at work with a gigantic coffee cake. Everyone in the office scolded him, but his smile remained nonetheless. "This is a special coffee cake," he explained. "I accidentally drove by the bakery this morning and there in the window was a host of goodies. I felt it was no accident, so I prayed, 'Lord, if you want me to have one of those delicious coffee cakes, let there be a parking spot open right in front.' And sure enough, the eighth time around the block, there it was!"

All of us know what it is to enter the wilderness of temptation. Temptation is part and parcel of the human condition. And we ourselves do an injustice as Christians when we overlook the seriousness of this topic. Temptation is like a wedge. In the world of physics, the mechanical world, there is hardly a more powerful application than a wedge. Once you get its thin edge in, it's just a matter of time and force how far that wedge will be able to split things apart. The hardest stone, the toughest bit of wood, no matter what, is not able to resist the power of a wedge to drive things apart. That's what temptation is like — the wedge that seeks to drive us apart from God.

And so the good news for us this morning is that we do not have to give in to temptation. There is One who has faced the tempter and defeated him. One who stands ready to come to our aid; One who promises to strengthen us in our times of temptation.

Our Scripture reading this morning recounts for us Jesus' encounter with the devil, the temptations he faced, and his triumph over them. Immediately after his baptism, Jesus was led by the Spirit into the wilderness to be tempted by the devil. It was not the only time Jesus would face temptation. In fact, throughout his life and ministry Jesus faced temptation. He was tempted to abandon the mission his Father in heaven had given him. He was tempted to go his own way. He was tempted to trust in his own power. But throughout his life, he was able to face temptation without falling; he was able to endure without sinning. And the question for us this morning is: What can we learn from Jesus about dealing with temptation? What help can Christ give us in our battle with that power that seeks to drive us away from God?

These are important questions for us to consider because temptation is one of those things that unite all of us. We are all tempted. Sin, temptation, and the power of the devil have open season on the children of God every single day of the year. In fact, it seems that the closer to God we wish to be, the more we seek to live our lives by faith, the more temptation plagues us. Jesus knew this. And that's why he taught his disciples to pray, "Lead us not into temptation." It's one thing to pray for forgiveness, but it's quite another to express our desire to live the Christian life by praying, "Lord, keep me from being tested beyond my power to resist."

Someone has said that opportunity knocks only once. It's temptation that keeps banging on your door! Jesus knew the power of temptation over the human heart and so he taught his disciples how to deal with it. Listen as he instructs the disciples on the night he was betrayed. Luke writes, "And he came out, and went, as was his custom, to the Mount of Olives; and the disciples followed him. And when he came to the place he said to them, 'Pray that you may not enter into temptation.' " Notice the linkage between prayer and temptation.

What follows then in Luke's gospel is a description of Jesus' own battle with temptation. It is here that Jesus himself prays, "Father, if thou art willing, remove this cup from me ... But not my will, O Lord, but Thine be done." His prayer is a prayer that God would give him strength to do what God required of him. That God would deliver him in that time of struggle. Luke's description of this prayer leaves no doubt as to the struggle that our Lord faced. Luke writes, "And his sweat became like great drops of blood falling down on the ground." Jesus knew what it was like to battle temptation. There, before the cross, his humanity was engaged in a great contest with his divinely appointed task.

It is interesting to note that when Jesus returned to the disciples that night at Gethsemane, he found them asleep, and when he woke them, he instructed them once again, "Rise and pray that you may not enter into temptation." There is a link between prayer and temptation. Jesus is telling us here that the first step in dealing with temptation is to pray — pray, first and foremost, that we may not even experience temptation. For temptation is the devil's way of leading us away from life.

M. Scott Peck, the author of the book *The Road Less Traveled,* once observed that the word "evil" is "live" spelled backwards. Temptation is the devil's way of turning things around, of leading us away from life. For when we enter into temptation, we walk away from life, we choose behavior that is anti-life, we fall into habits that are not healthy, and we expose ourselves to influences that are anything but good, wholesome and lasting. "Pray," Jesus says, "that you may not even enter into temptation."

We snicker when the actress in the musical *Oklahoma* sings, "I'm just a girl who can't say no." We smirk at Zsa Zsa Gabor, who says, "To sin is human; it just feels divine." However, in a day and age when sinfulness is shown as everyday, acceptable behavior on television, when lives are corrupted by the expanding gambling industry, when thousands of people, young and old, lose their lives to alcohol and drug-related deaths, it is time for us to take the power of the devil and temptation seriously.

For you see, most of us can handle the big crises of life. It is temptation, the little "foxes that eat the vines" (as Solomon noted thousands of years ago) that give us the trouble. Bobby Leach, an Englishman, startled the world early in the 1920s by going over Niagara Falls in a barrel, escaping serious harm. However, few people know that he spent the last years of his life as an invalid, after he slipped on an orange peel and broke his back. That's the way temptation works. It sneaks up on us, and if we don't watch out, if we live dependent upon our own power alone, temptation has the power to destroy us.

And that's why Jesus tells us that the first step in dealing with temptation is to pray. Pray that we may not be tempted, for temptation always leads us away from God. The second thing we need to do in dealing with temptation is to acknowledge that it has great power over us. We need God's help in dealing with temptation. We need to affirm that there is One whose power to deal with the tempter is greater than ours, One who can do battle with the devil and triumph. For without that One with us, we are sure to fail.

The sure antidote to temptation is to be focused on Christ, to be so filled with his power, his salvation, his life and service, that there is no room for temptation. Shortly after the Reformation, some young followers of Martin Luther wrote him (kind of like an original Ann Landers) with a question, saying, "We are harassed by many temptations which appeal to us so often and so strongly that they give us no rest. You don't seem to be troubled in this way and we should like to know your secret. Don't temptations bother you? Are you somehow immune to sin?"

Luther wrote them back in reply, saying, "I, too, know something of temptation. But the difference is that when temptation comes knocking at the door of my heart, I always answer, 'Go away! This place is occupied. Go back where you came from, for Christ is here.' "

The key to understanding and dealing with temptation is found in those words: "for Christ is here." There is another law of physics that says that a vacuum will always be filled by whatever is near it. And so it is with our hearts. They will be filled with whatever is around us. How many people have found themselves led into heartache and patterns of unholy living simply by the friends they kept and the places they visited? How many have drifted away from God and the church because they occupied themselves with unwholesome music, movies, television, or just plain old lazy living?

Martin Luther told those youthful followers of his that the key to dealing with temptation was to allow Christ to fill their hearts. Give God room in your heart and when God fills your heart, there will be little room left for temptation. And it begins with prayer: prayer that asks God to help us overcome temptation; prayer that keeps us focused on Christ; prayer that trusts that God will strengthen and guide us. For if our prayers are that God strengthen and deliver us from temptation, we shall prevail. For Romans 10:13 says, "Everyone who calls on the name of the Lord will be saved."

God is faithful; our prayers will be answered. We will be strengthened to overcome even the most persistent temptation. Now, that may not happen instantly. It may not even happen as we expect it. But prayer is the key to dealing with temptation. There is a legend about Monica, the mother of Augustine. She prayed that God would block her son's trip to Italy. Monica, a devout Christian, was worried about her son. She saw him throwing his life away and was concerned that the trip to Rome would only harm him further. She was sure that there he would fall further from God into sinful living and never come to believe in Christ.

But while she was praying that God prevent him from traveling there, Augustine sailed off. She thought she had lost.

But while Augustine was there in Rome, God worked a great miracle in his life. For after he arrived there, he met and fell under the influence of the mighty preacher Ambrose and became a Christian — in the very place that his mother was praying that he would not go.

We have to be careful with our prayers. We dare not use our prayers to give God orders, because perhaps the ultimate temptation is to think that we know more than God does, that we care more than God cares, that we see the future better than God. Our prayers must always be that we depend upon God to strengthen us and that we trust God to lead us not into temptation.

Dear friends, Lent is a time to send the devil a message. Look around you. What kind of friends are you keeping? What kind of places do you frequent? What does your checkbook say about the way you spend your life? We have six weeks ahead of us — six weeks to say to the devil, "Go away from me. This place is taken. Christ is already here." Amen.

Who Lives
In You?

Who lives in you? That's the question that comes to mind as we read those words of Jesus this morning when he tells the Pharisees, "Go tell that fox (Herod) that I will drive out demons and heal people today and tomorrow and on the third day reach my goal." I will do what I must. For God lives in me. I am a citizen of heaven. Let him do what he must!

Let your imagination run free for a moment and picture yourself, your personality, who you are really, as a house. Any kind of house will do — just so it's yours. For some it may be a huge castle, with lofty turrets and banners waving in the breeze, a place that is safe and secure. For others it may be a rustic cabin, tucked away in the woods, a peaceful and quiet refuge. For others still, it might be a nice little retirement home, with a rocking chair on the front porch, a shade tree in front and a nice warm breeze stirring flowers blooming in front.

Now, move in closer and imagine the front door of that house. Picture someone pushing the doorbell, clanking the knocker, or rapping on the door. If someone came to the door of your house, who would they find inside? Who lives in you?

I'm not sure about you, but I've met people who gave me the distinct impression that if I went inside the "houses" of their lives, I wouldn't find anyone home. Or if I went inside their houses, they would be so cluttered with junk that there wouldn't be any room for anyone. Or some whose houses are great and impressive on the outside, but once I entered everything would be artificial.

Who lives in you? That's the question for us to address this Second Sunday in Lent. Who lives in you? What guides your decisions? What sets the course of your life? What determines the way you think and treat others around you? Most of us would like to say that it is our Christian faith that determines who we are. But is that so? For there are two kinds of people who can be home — citizens of the world and citizens of heaven.

Who lives in you? Think back over the decisions you've made this past week. Who made them — a citizen of this world or a citizen of heaven? Recall the way you spoke to those around you and the way you treated others. Who was present then? What about the offering you bring this morning, what kind of relationship with God does it reflect? Is it a citizen of heaven, the child of God, who is present in us? Or is it a stranger of this world, one who cares little about others, who thinks first of him or herself, whose actions fail to give witness to the allegiance we claim to have with God?

Who lives in you? What stirs you each day of your life? We'd like to answer that it is our Christian faith, but can we? For the Christian faith is more than just a set of doctrines, more than some creed that we recite, more than assertions we study. Our Christian faith is the lives we live — the set of moral principles that guide our decisions and are reflected in the words we use. It is our response to the poor around us. It is our record of worship, our interest in Scripture reading, our attention to prayer.

For the reality of our Christian faith is our relationship with Christ, the same kind of response that Jesus gave those Pharisees. "Look and see how I act," he said. "See, I go about my business. I will continue to care for the sick and proclaim God's Word." Who lives in you? The answer must always be "Christ lives in me." The same love, the same compassion that Jesus had is present in me. The same life, the same power of God that was present in Jesus is alive in me. I am a citizen of heaven. God is my Father. And it is up to me to live according to that citizenship. I cannot say I am a citizen of heaven, a child of God, and make myself a stranger to the house of God. I cannot say I am a citizen of heaven and live as an "undercover agent," afraid someone during the week will discover my true identity.

This Season of Lent calls us to look within ourselves and ask the question: "Who lives in me?" It calls us to be honest with ourselves and admit that even though we claim to be citizens of heaven, we often live as strangers before God.

A researcher for a publishing company recently interviewed a number of people to determine what kind of books they liked to read. Among the most common answers were: the Bible, Shakespeare, and a number of classic works such as *A Tale of Two Cities, The Red Badge of Courage*, and others. In return for their cooperation, the company offered each person a choice of a free book from a list of titles published by the company. There was a large variety of books to choose from, ranging from Christian devotional books to classical titles, and some of more recent authors. It was interesting to note that the most popular choice of this supposedly high-minded group of readers was *The Murder of a Burlesque Queen.*

Sometimes we claim to be citizens of heaven and yet live as strangers to God because we think no one will notice the difference. After all, we are not as bad as others around us, are we? And we do bring an offering to church, even though it may be less than we spend weekly on entertainment. And we do plan on reading our Bibles and saying our prayers, sometime, don't we? How often we live as strangers to God and try to claim we are citizens of heaven and hope no one notices the difference.

But the Season of Lent reminds us that God knows. That we may be able to fool ourselves (and even those around us) but we can never fool God, for God reads the human heart. God knows who lives in our house.

There is a story of a burly, old lineman from a professional football team who thought that he knew all the tricks so he could stay out late and party on road trips despite the team's curfew. Over the years he'd gotten it all down to a science. He'd pile certain things up under the blankets of the bed to make it appear that he was asleep when the coach checked curfew. And it worked fairly well until one evening when he was in a hurry and couldn't find the right items to put under the covers, so he just decided to slip a floor lamp under the blankets instead. Imagine what happened when a suspicious coach peeked in at 1 a.m. and snapped on the poor guy's light.

The cross of Jesus is like that. It lays bare the thoughts of the human heart and reveals the inner person. Who lives in you? If you want to know the answer to that question, review your thoughts and actions in the light of the cross. How does your life reflect Jesus' love? How do your actions make God's compassion more visible? Who lives in you?

Jesus tells us that two kinds of people cannot live in peace with each other. "No one can serve two masters," he says. Either we live as people whose lives are oriented to the world, who strive for happiness and fulfillment in the things of this world, who find our joy in the pleasures, pursuits, and possessions of this life, or we find our peace and joy in Christ. Both kinds of people cannot live under the same roof.

Dwight Moody tells a story about two inebriated men who found their way back to the dock one night after a long night of partying. They were relieved to find the boat still there. They decided to try to make it home. So they got in and began to row. They rowed hard in what was left of the night, but when the sun came up, they were dismayed to discover that they were in exactly the same spot where they had started. For in their drunken state they had forgotten to untie the mooring line and raise the anchor.

We cannot live with our hopes and dreams, our aspirations and goals for life tied to the material possessions of this world and yet claim to be citizens of heaven. We cannot live dividing our priorities between serving ourselves and serving God. We cannot live as citizens of heaven and be strangers to God. Jesus says, "Either you will hate the one and love the other or be devoted to the one and despise the other. No one can serve two masters." It is impossible to hold dual citizenship.

To be a child of God is to allow God to be our Father. To live as a citizen of heaven is to allow Christ into our hearts. For when we have the love of Jesus in our hearts, we know a life of discipleship and devotion, of faith and faithfulness, of conscience and commitment will follow. But we must allow Christ in! We must allow the love of God to rule our lives, direct our thoughts, and guide our actions.

In his autobiography, Dr. A.J. Cronin tells of a neighboring family called the Adamses. Mr. Adams was an accountant in New York City, but he loved to spend all the hours he could working in his garden at their Connecticut home with his only son, Sammy. When WWII broke out, Mrs. Adams suggested they take a refugee child into their home. Mr. Adams wasn't much in favor of the idea, but he went along with it to please her. The child they received came from an orphanage in Central Europe with the impossible name of Paul Piotrostansilis. Unfortunately, as Paul learned the language of his new family in Connecticut, he also learned to manipulate the truth. He found it easy to steal and do mischief and broke the Adams' hearts many times. He did, however, develop a close friendship with the Adams' little son, Sammy.

One day, Paul, against their specific warning, went swimming in a polluted stream near their home and came back with an infection that brought with it a raging fever. Because of the possibility it might be contagious, Paul was put in a separate room and Sammy was told to stay away from him. Paul eventually pulled through the crisis, but, while he was still sick, one morning the family found Sammy asleep in bed with Paul, the two of them breathing into each other's faces. And sure enough, Sammy caught the disease. The fever raged through him, and only four days later, Sammy died.

Dr. Cronin remembered hearing about the tragedy while away on an extended study leave. He wrote his neighbors, expressing his sympathy for them, telling them that he, for one, would understand should they feel the need to send Paul back, after all the heartache he had caused them. A few months later, upon returning from his leave, Dr. Cronin went next door to visit the Adamses and was surprised to see the same familiar sight of a man and a boy working side by side in the garden. Only this time the boy was Paul.

"You still have him then?" Cronin inquired. "Yes," Henry Adams replied, "and he is doing much better now." "All I can say to you, Paul," Cronin muttered, "is that you're a pretty lucky boy." "Dr. Cronin," Henry interrupted, "you don't need to bother trying to pronounce his name anymore, either. He is now Paul Adams. We have adopted him. He is now the son we lost."

That's the kind of love God has for us. A love that Jesus expresses in the face of threatened death, a love that goes about its business, in spite of the consequences. Love that adopts us as children. Love that makes us citizens of heaven. Love that puts us in our places and gives us our inheritances. Who lives in you? May we all be able to say, "Christ lives in me for I live in him." Amen.

Yes,
But How?

Lent 3   *Luke 13:1-9*

A friend of mine tells a story about a man who borrowed a book from an acquaintance. As he read through it, he was intrigued to find parts of the book underlined with the letters YBH written in the margin. When he returned the book to the owner, he asked what the YBH meant. The owner replied that the underlined paragraphs were sections of the book that he basically agreed with. They gave him hints on how to improve himself and pointed out truths that he wished to incorporate into his life. However, the letters YBH stood for "Yes, but how?"

And that's the question for us this morning: "Yes, but how?" "I ought to know how to take better care of myself, but how?" "I know I ought to spend more time in scripture reading and prayer, but how?" "I know I ought to be more sensitive to others, more loving of my spouse, more understanding of the weaknesses of others, but how?" These are all good qualities and we know that, but how can we acquire them? As Christian people we know the kind of life we ought to live, and most of us have the best of intentions to do so, but how? We are afraid because we know where the road paved with only good intentions leads!

This morning we hear Jesus' parable of the fig tree, telling us to repent and bear good fruit. We know what the Christian life requires of us and yet, if we are honest with ourselves, we also know how far short we fall. So the question that confronts us this morning is: "Yes, but how?"

It's a dilemma that has confronted God's people throughout the ages. Even Saint Paul found himself trapped. In Romans 7 Paul writes:

> *It seems to be a fact of life that when I want to do what is right, I inevitably do what is wrong. I love to do God's will so far as my new (redeemed Christian) nature is concerned; but there is something else deep within me, in my lower nature, that is at war with my mind and wins the fight and makes me a slave to the sin that is still within me. In my mind, I want to be God's willing servant, but instead I find myself enslaved to sin. So you see how it is; my new life (the redeemed life in Christ) tells me to do right, but the old nature that is still inside me (my sinful human self) loves to sin. Oh, what a terrible predicament I'm in! Who will free me from this slavery to sin? Thank God! It has already been done by Jesus Christ our Lord. He has set me free!*

"Repent," Jesus says. "Acknowledge your sinfulness." That's the first step in beginning to live the Christian life. None of us is without fault. And yet how difficult it is for us to admit that. We know better than to openly admit our wrongs. If we want to get ahead in this world and be accepted by others, it's generally better to conceal our shortcomings and put on a good front for others.

Who goes into a job interview and declares, "I have to tell you. I have a habit of missing work, of criticizing my supervisors and others, and I enjoy listening to office gossip?" Who goes on a date and confesses to the other person, "Listen. I have to tell you I tend to be difficult to live with and I can be a real bore at times"?

However imperfect we may be, we've learned from life around us that it's better not to parade our imperfections out in public. As the little girl said to her classmate who had to sit in the corner, "To err is human, but to admit it is just plain stupid!"

How ironic it is then, that Jesus would tell us to repent. Instead of offering a word of support and understanding for our all-too-

26

human tendency to cover up our wrongdoings, Jesus tells us to disclose the evil within us, to admit that we have failed. The apostle John tells us the same thing very clearly when he writes, "If we say we have no sin, we deceive ourselves and the truth is not in us."

Whoever we are, whatever we do, we all share one thing in common and that is that we are sinful. Saint Augustine once wrote, "Whatever we are, we are not what we ought to be." Mark Twain, with his characteristic sense of humor, tells us how he understands that when he wrote, "Man was made at the end of the week, when God was tired."

Repent, Jesus says, for that's the first step in the Christian life. Confess your sins before God and receive God's forgiveness. In that sense, confession *is* good for the soul, true confession, not the kind of glib admission that says, "Sure I've sinned. Who hasn't?" True confession that begins with a heartfelt remorse, a feeling of failure to live up to God's love and a desire to reform. "Blessed are those who mourn," Jesus said, and part of what he was speaking about is those who feel the pain of a guilty conscience and grieve in the awareness that we have failed to live up to the expectations of God and those around us.

Confession is good for the soul — yes, we know that — but how can we develop a true sense of heartfelt remorse for our sinfulness and a real desire to change our ways? Most of us are willing to confess our sins as long as we don't have to change. We are willing to admit to a blemish or two on our moral complexion but nothing that can not be cosmetically covered up with a coating of good manners. None of us wants to admit that our sinfulness may require reconstructive surgery! After all, we like to think that God is happy with us the way we are and really only wants to make us happy with ourselves.

We think this because most of us never take seriously the concept of sin. I read recently an article about the difficulty a translator had in rendering the Bible into an African dialect. It seemed that the particular language had no suitable term for "sin." Apparently the people who spoke that dialect lacked the concept. The closest the translator could come up with was a word that meant "something bad to eat."

For a lot of people that's the extent of it. Sin is a matter of taste. So what if "we are what we eat"? Taste is an individual matter and nobody has the right to tell another what to like or not like. And if sin is just a matter of taste, it certainly doesn't require the radical solution of repentance. It's easy for us to conclude that we aren't truly bad when we compare ourselves to others. There are plenty of people worse than us.

But the truth of our moral and spiritual condition becomes evident only when we compare ourselves to Jesus. In the light of his life, our lives look awful! Sure, terrible wrongdoing, grisly crimes, sins of passion and violence may not be part of our personal history — but what about our neglect of the poor, our passive acceptance of injustice toward others, our silence in the face of hurtful gossip, our failure to reverence God as we ought? When we look at our lives in the light of Jesus' love, even our best, our righteousness is, as the Scriptures tell us, like "filthy rags."

Confession is good for the soul, we know that, and it is the first step in beginning to live the Christian life, and the recognition that without God we are incomplete. Sin is not a matter of taste. It is sampling the forbidden fruit. It is taking poison into our lives, and the only antidote for sin is repentance. We need to repent of our sinfulness, receive God's forgiveness, and produce the fruit that God desires. We need the spiritual strength and renewal the confession can give us.

Remember, Jesus is not demanding anything that we cannot produce. He doesn't ask the fig tree to produce bananas. He doesn't expect the fig tree to grow tall as an oak or be fragrant as a cedar. He is only asking it to be what it is, to do what it ought: produce figs. You and I have differing gifts. Some have wonderful singing voices. Others have graceful bodies. Some are artists, others are good with numbers, and others still are good with people. Each of us has our own unique gifts. And the miracle that happens is that through repentance and forgiveness, those gifts are released for the good of God and others around us.

When we acknowledge our sinfulness and receive God's forgiveness, God releases us from the power of sin. And only when we are free from sin do we have the possibility to become who God has created us to be — children of God, young and old, each able to produce the fruits of faith. Remember Saint Paul's words: "What a terrible predicament I am in! Who will free me from this slavery to sin? Thank God! It has already been done by Jesus Christ my Lord. He has set me free."

That's the key to our dilemma, the answer to our question, "Yes, but how?" How do we live the life of faith we are called to live as followers of Christ? How can we do what we ought to do? The key to living the life "worthy of our calling" as children of God is to remember that God has already set us free! In Christ Jesus I am free! I am free to be who God has made me to be. It is up to me to get on with it. I only need allow Christ to live in me and take control of my life.

Sometimes we think that when we give up control of our lives to Christ, we are no longer responsible for them. But just the opposite is true. When we turn our lives over to God, allow Christ to direct us, then we become truly responsible for ourselves.

Jesus' parable of the fig tree calls us to take responsibility for ourselves, for God gives us the key. Repent, Jesus says. Confess your sins and allow the power of God to live within you. Allow God to enable us to live as we ought. Let Jesus take possession of us and live in him.

Fritz Kreisler, the great violinist, expresses it this way. He says, "I have not the slightest consciousness of what my fingers are doing when I play. I concentrate on the ideal of the music that I hear in my head and I try to come as near to that as I can. I don't think of the mechanics at all. You might say that a musician who has to think of the mechanics is not ready for public performance yet."

That's what Saint Paul is trying to tell us. The violinist's fingers may still make a mistake now and then, just as we may still make mistakes as we live out our lives. But when our hearts and minds are tied to the Spirit of Christ, when we have been released from sin by repentance and forgiveness, when we hold steady the example of Jesus in our lives, our hearts and minds will move the melody of God's love. The key, however, begins with repentance and confession. For there we receive the release we need, there we are filled with the power of forgiveness, there we find the answer to the question that plagues us, "Yes, but how?" In Jesus' name, of course. Amen.

Playboy Or Plowboy —
Let The Party Begin

Lent 4   *Luke 15:1-3, 11b-32*

It's a story that we all know by heart, the story of the father and his two sons. One was a plowboy, who stayed home, behaved himself and enjoyed the good life. The other was a playboy, who sought for himself the good life and ended up in a pigpen. Reduced to abject misery, the playboy swallowed his pride and came home, to be welcomed with a great celebration of joy.

The plowboy was angry at his father and jealous of his brother, so he boycotted the party. Coming in late from the fields, he heard music the likes of which he had never heard before coming from the house. It was a servant who explained to him, "Your brother has come home and your father has killed the fatted calf." And, boy, was he mad.

I don't know, maybe the plowboy was fattening the calf for the county fair. But more likely, he was angry that the calf was killed for his no-good playboy brother. And although the dominant mood on the farm that night was one of joy and celebration, there was at least one who was not so happy — the plowboy brother. So unhappy, in fact, that he decided not only to boycott the party, but to spill his misery on as many people as he could, to wither the lettuce of their joy with the hot grease of his bitterness.

But thank God the plowboy and the playboy are not the only two characters in the story. There is also the loving father, the father who loved his sons with a deep, abiding love. And in spite of the great joy he had over the return of his long-lost son, he would not let it eclipse his love for the elder brother. And so the father came out and reminded his son of the good life they enjoyed together. The father left the warmth of the celebration joy and went into the cold night of the plowboy son's self-imposed pity.

It just wasn't fair — was his complaint. In spite of his accumulated seniority on the farm, there had never been a time when even a lean goat (much less a fatted calf) had been slaughtered for him. It wasn't fair! But the father had his turn to speak and the father countered his son's brokenness and gives us our text for this morning. "Son," he says, "you are always with me, and all that is mine is yours!"

What an amazing story, this parable of the Prodigal Son. For there's more to it than just the story of a runaway boy. For each and every one of us, it is the story of our lives as well! *Runaway or rebellious* — who cannot remember a time when one was at odds with parents, distanced from God or just "away from home" where one knew one ought not be? Or *disciplined and disgruntled* — who cannot remember a time when doing right, fulfilling the expectations, staying at home seemed overlooked and unappreciated. This story of the playboy and the plowboy puts us in our places and shows us the Father.

For like most of the parables of Jesus, this story is a picture of God. A God who loves us enough to let go. The parable is the story of the playboy, the rebellious young man who goes to his father and demands his inheritance, only to squander it away. And when he returns, the father welcomes him home. In that sense, it is the story of a God who loves us enough to let go and to welcome us home in forgiveness when we return.

But it is also a story of a God who provides in abundance, whose love and care surround us each day. For it is also the story of the plowboy and a father who loves him with a constant love. The story tells us that sometimes the good life can become commonplace. The thousands of times the plowboy sat at his father's table had taken the edge off the blessing. It was no longer his father's providing that he enjoyed at home, but the wages he had earned for the work he had done. The plowboy's problem was that in his resentment over the fatted calf roasting on the spit, he had forgotten the deep freezer full of provisions that he constantly enjoyed. He'd forgotten the many times he had sat at the family table and was nourished by its delicious delights.

The story tells us that sometimes God's blessings can become commonplace and when they do, it is easy for us to miss the ordinary because we are only looking for the spectacular. For if we are not careful, like the plowboy, we have a tendency to see the Father's blessings at only the high points of our lives and forget the millions of bite-sized blessings we enjoy continually throughout our lives.

It can happen to us and it happened to the plowboy. His perspective was distorted by ingratitude. He had worked hard, he had earned everything he had received. It was not the father's to give — it was his right! And so when he saw the incredible generosity of the father, he was enraged and his perspective was distorted. Listen to the conversation he had with his father. After the father left the party to come out to him, the plowboy began to file his complaint. And he zeroed in on his unhappiness when he said (and listen carefully), "When this son of yours," (notice he says *son of yours*), "when this son of yours came back, who had devoured your property with prostitutes, you killed the fatted calf for him." The amazing thing about this is that what he said is true. The playboy was wrong. No doubt about it. He had squandered the inheritance. He had brought dishonor on the family. He had "sinned against God and man," as he readily admitted.

The plowboy's problem, however, was not that he had his facts mixed up. It was a matter of perspective — a problem of attitude. In his self-conceived pity, his poor-me perspective, he could not see the same love and forgiveness, that the same welcome that meant the father had found a long lost SON also meant that he had received a long lost BROTHER. And so the father had to explain, saying, "We had to celebrate and rejoice because this *brother of yours* was dead and has come to life."

Two siblings — one who wasted his inheritance on wild and destructive living — and the other who could not welcome his brother back. Two people who were both wrong: the younger who turned his back on his father and the elder who turned his back on his brother. And neither is worse than the other.

Let me tell you a true story. Back in 1893 there were a group of four sisters, the Cherry Sisters they called themselves, who made their stage debut in Cedar Rapids in a skit they wrote themselves. For three years, the Cherry Sisters performed to packed theaters throughout the Midwest. People came to see them to find out if they were as bad as they had heard. Their unbelievably atrocious acting enraged critics and provoked the audience to throw vegetables at the would-be actresses. Wisely, the sisters thought it best to travel with an iron screen which they would erect in front of the stage in self-defense.

Amazingly, in 1896 the girls were offered a thousand dollars a week to perform on Broadway — not because they were so good, but because they were so unbelievably bad. Seven years later, after the Cherry Sisters had earned what in that day was a respectable fortune of $200,000, they retired from the stage for the peaceful life back on the farm. Oddly enough, these successful Broadway "stars" remained convinced to the end that they were truly the most talented actresses ever to grace the American stage. They never had a clue as to how bad they truly were!

The parable this morning does not tell us what the elder brother did when his father came out to speak to him. It doesn't reveal to us whether the plowboy realized his envy and disdain had made him just as bad as the playboy. Yes, the elder brother had never stooped to find himself in the pigpens of life. He would never have been caught dead carousing with prostitutes or wasting his resources in riotous living (and that's good!). Even though he had no right to judge, he could not understand what caused his brother to leave. He would not accept the sincerity of his brother's confession and was scandalized at his father's joy and welcome. In the end, his inability to forgive, his refusal to rejoice at the return of another were just as offensive to Jesus as the sins of the playboy.

This parable is a story about God, our God, who loves us with an everlasting love and accepts us, playboy and plowboy alike. It is a story of ourselves. You and I know many elder brothers in this world. In fact, we are often them. And we have trouble accepting those whom God accepts, forgiving those whom God forgives, and loving those whom God loves.

Perhaps you've seen the cartoon strip, *Calvin and Hobbes*. Calvin is a little boy with an overactive imagination and a stuffed tiger, Hobbes, who comes to life as his imaginary friend. In one cartoon strip, Calvin turns to his friend Hobbes and says, "I feel bad I called Susie names and hurt her feelings. I'm sorry I did that." Hobbes replies, "Maybe you should apologize to her." Calvin thinks about it for a moment and then responds, "I keep hoping there's a less obvious solution." We have trouble accepting those whom God accepts because we take God's acceptance for granted and God's forgiveness as our right.

We are much like the elder brother who preferred justice to mercy. We have worked for what we have (or so we think), and it's unfair that everyone else should not have to do the same. We have earned God's favor (or so we think) by "staying at home." We have merited his acceptance by the good life that we live. So how dare God receive and accept the playboy who returns with repentance? We forget that the reason Jesus told this story to begin with was to remind those for whom God's favor had become commonplace that God's love encompasses everyone and that God's forgiveness and welcome are open to all. For the fact is, we are all sinners, whether we stay at home or wander away. We are all sinners, whether we turn our backs on God or on our brothers or sisters in righteous judgment of them.

Yes, God treats God's children differently. Jesus tells us that in the parable of the talents where one person is given ten talents of gold, another three and yet another only one. When the master returns, the master commends those who used their talents and rebuked the one who did not. And the conclusion of the parable says, "For everyone who has been given much, much is required."

God treats all differently, but loves all the same, with an everlasting love that forgives the wayward and welcomes the prodigal, as well as continually blesses those at home. Some of us here this morning may identify with the prodigal. We can acknowledge that there are things in our lives that we regret, times when we let others down, broken promises, failed actions, and sins of which we are

35

not proud. The story this morning tells us that there is a place at God's table for us.

Others may identify with the elder brother. For even a quick review of our lives shows us times when we passed judgment on others, times when we looked down on others, exalted ourselves in our righteousness, and despised the sinner who did not measure up. The story this morning tells us that there's a place at God's table for us as well. Playboy or plowboy — God's welcome awaits us. His forgiveness is real and his love eternal. So let the party begin. It is time for us to turn in repentance, accept the Father's welcome and come to God's table of grace. Amen.

Forgiven!

On a recent religious talk show the hostess was interviewing a young woman who had just recently come to know Christ and had been received into the church. Until her recent conversion, she had lived on the wrong side of the tracks, lived in the fast lane, and teetered on the brink of destruction. So overwhelming was the sense of forgiveness that this young woman practically gushed with joy as she spoke. "I can't express," she said, "the sense of gratitude that I feel that God has changed my life."

The talk show hostess knew where she was coming from — for she, too, had walked on life's wild side before coming to Jesus. She said, "I know what you mean. Every day I thank God for saving me!" And then she added a very profound statement: "You know what I've noticed though? People who have always been in the church, people who always do what they ought, who have never really gotten into trouble, always been prim and proper, don't have the same sense of gratitude that I do. In fact, I've noticed that for most church people, it's not so much what God had done for them, but what they still want God to do!"

If you can identify with that statement, perhaps we can appreciate the story in today's Gospel reading from John 12. It's an unusual story — this story of the anointing of Jesus' feet with oil. All four Gospel writers include it in their writing, but only

John records it as happening in the house of Mary, Martha, and Lazarus. Matthew, Mark, and Luke tell essentially the same story (in fact, most Bible commentators agree that it is the same story). However, in the first three Gospels, the woman who anoints Jesus' feet is not identified as Mary, but simply identified as "a woman of the city, a sinner." The meal takes place not in Bethany, but at the home of a Pharisee. And instead of Judas objecting to the waste of the money for the perfume, it was a Pharisee who was scandalized by a sinful woman touching Jesus. But essentially the story is the same. Jesus sums it up when he concludes, "Therefore I tell you, her sins, which are many, are forgiven, for she loved much, but he who is forgiven little, loves little."

Forgiven — that's the theme of today's Gospel reading — good news for broken hearts — God's forgiveness can cover us all. Theologian Karl Barth knew this. He once declared, "We live solely by forgiveness." He was but echoing the message of the apostle Paul. Paul knew what it was to struggle with forgiveness. He once wrote that he knew the law better than any and that he had struggled mightily to obey it, for he believed it to be the way of salvation. But instead of saving him, instead of soothing his hurting heart, it only condemned him. And Saint Paul was not alone in that conclusion. Many a person has felt that way. Martin Luther wrestled with the same difficulty until he came to discover a loving God, a God of forgiveness and love.

We are forgiven. We are made right not by our own efforts, but by One whose death pays the price for our sins. As Paul put it in Galatians 2:21: "I am not one of those who treats Christ's death as meaningless. For if we could be saved by keeping the Jewish laws, then there is no need for Christ to die" (Living Bible).

Forgiven! Can you grasp the full meaning of that word? In today's Gospel reading, Mary did and that's why she offered the burial perfume in loving service to Jesus. That's why the woman in the Gospels of Matthew, Mark, and Luke anointed Jesus' feet with oil and washed them with her hair. Such was the depth of her gratitude for the gift of forgiveness. Forgiven! Have you felt that power? Mark Twain once said that everyone is like the moon — we each have a dark side which never shows and no one can see.

But God knows the darkness within us. God knows the shameful thoughts, the hidden actions, the unkind words, and the careless deeds that are part of all of our lives. And yet because of what Jesus did on the cross, God accepts us just as we are, dark side and all!

All of our sins — all of our transgressions, all of our sinful acts and thoughts — are completely drowned in the sea of God's forgiveness. Some Christians pray, "Forgive us our trespasses." Others say, "Forgive us our debts." And still others say, "Forgive us our sins." Whatever the words, the meaning is the same. We come to God in need of forgiveness — forgiveness for what we have done — and the strength to forgive others.

All too many Christians operate with an Old Testament view of God. For them, God is a God of judgment, a God of vengeance and wrath. As far as these Christians are concerned, Jesus need never have come. For they do not need his forgiveness, they do not need God's grace.

In one of his books, Alan Paton, the great South African writer, tells a powerful story which takes place before the recent changes in South Africa. In the story a white police lieutenant falls in love with a black African woman. Not only was it against the laws of apartheid in that stern, racist society, but also it was an abominable sin, an unforgivable offense.

The lieutenant is confronted by his captain and initially denies the charge, but the evidence is so overwhelming that he is forced to confess his transgression. Then the captain does what appears to be a strange thing. He goes to visit the lieutenant's father and reports the situation to him. What follows is a moving and tragic scene.

The father asks the captain, "Is it true?" The captain replies, "I fear it is." The father insists, "Are you sure?" And the captain answers, "He confessed it to me. It must be true." The father stands unmoving, the silence broken only by his heavy breathing, like some creature in agonizing pain. In the room observing the scene are the father's wife and his sister. He turns to his sister and says to her, "Bring me the Book." She goes to the bookcase, pulls down the heavy family Bible and sets it on the table in front of him. As she puts it on the table, she wonders aloud what passage he is going to read.

But he doesn't read any passage at all. Instead he opens the front of the book where the family names have been recorded for 150 years. He takes the pen and ink and crosses out the name of his son, Peter van Vlaanderen, not once but many times as though to completely obliterate it from the page. Without any anger or despair (at least none that anyone sees), without any words, and without any emotion, he does away with his son. Then he turns to the captain and very calmly asks, "Is there anything more?" The captain knows this is his cue to leave and he does, offering to the mother and aunt any help he can give them. But the father turns abruptly to him and says, "No one in this house will ask for help!" So the captain leaves. The father, still sitting at the table, turns to his sister and says, "Lock the door and bolt it and bring me the key. The door of our house will never open again." That's the scene. The door is closed forever. The son can never return home.

That is NOT the picture of God that Jesus brings us. You are forgiven, Jesus tells us. You are forgiven and set free. And instead of our names being obliterated from the Book of Life, Jesus writes them with indelible ink! You are forgiven and given a new start in life. That's what the word "forgiveness" means. The word "repent" appears 46 times in the Old Testament. Did you know that in 37 of those instances it is God who is said to repent? Now "repent" must mean more than just to be sorry for our sins. For no one would say that God needs to be sorry for his sin. No — repentance means to have a change of mind, a change of attitude, a change of direction. To know that the slate is wiped clean calls for a new start, and that's what God's forgiveness does for us. It offers us a new start.

A new start, knowing that we are forgiven, then gives us the power to offer forgiveness to others. If we know ourselves as sinners made acceptable to God only by the grace of Jesus Christ, how can we possibly refuse to forgive another? It is impossible. George Whitefield was one of the greatest evangelists that ever lived. He was a true man of God, and yet when he saw a condemned man going to the gallows he whispered the famous words, "There but for the grace of God go I." George knew the truth of Barth's words, "We all live by forgiveness." For forgiveness allows us to accept the love that God has for us.

Could that have been Judas' greatest downfall, the inability to see himself as a sinner and hence receive God's forgiveness? For without that sense of forgiveness, life holds little joy and the future is hopeless. Someone once said that the person who knows himself or herself to be a sinner and does not know God's forgiveness is like an overweight person who fears stepping on a scale. You are forgiven, Jesus tells us. My cross is for you.

I once read about a very bitter man who was sick in soul, mind, and body. He was in the hospital in wretched condition, not because his body had been invaded by a virus or infected with some germ, but because his anger and contempt had poisoned his soul. One day, when he was at his lowest, he said to his nurse, "Won't you give me something to end it all?" Much to the man's surprise, the nurse said, "All right. I will." She went to the nightstand and pulled out the Gideon Bible and began to read, "For God so loved the world that he gave his only begotten Son that whosoever believeth in him should not perish but have eternal life." When she finished she said, "There, if you will believe that, it will end it all. God loves you, forgives you and accepts you as his child."

Such a simple answer may not work for everyone. But it worked for that man. He realized after much soul-searching that she had spoken truly. And over a period of some time, he came to believe and accept God's love for him.

There is a way to God. Jesus died to provide it. We may not be Mary or that "woman of the city," but there are sins that weigh upon our hearts. There are scars and cuts that we have inflicted on others. There is a darkness within each of us that no one knows of but God. But that same One, our loving God, sees all and forgives all and calls us to God.

Remember, the one who is forgiven little loves little. But the one who is forgiven much loves with all the heart! May that be true of us. In Jesus' name. Amen.

Cut Down
And Lifted Up

Passion/Palm Sunday   *Luke 23:1-49*

Let me tell you an ancient parable from the Orient.

Once upon a time in the heart of a certain kingdom, there lay a beautiful garden. And of all the dwellers in that garden, the most beautiful and beloved to the master of the garden was the noble Bamboo. Year after year, Bamboo grew yet more beautiful and lovely. Bamboo was conscious of the master's love, and yet he was still modest and in all things gentle.

Often the Wind would come and play a tune in the garden and Bamboo would cast aside his dignity and sway and dance merrily, tossing to and fro in wonderful abandon. And when he danced, the master who looked on was delighted and filled with joy.

One day the master came to the garden and approached Bamboo. Bamboo bowed his head and greeted the master with joy. And the master spoke, "Bamboo, I would use you." And when Bamboo heard those words, he leaped with joy for he knew that this was what his life was all about. "Master," Bamboo said, "I am ready. Use me if you will."

"Bamboo," the master said, his voice grave and serious. "I would be obliged to take you and cut you down." A trembling of great horror shook Bamboo. "Cut me down, Master? Cut me down? Me whom you have made the most beautiful in all your garden? Cut me down? Oh, no! Not that. Take me and use me, if you wish, but do not cut me down."

"Beloved Bamboo," the master said, "if I do not cut you down, I cannot use you." The garden grew still. The Wind held her breath. Bamboo, proud and glorious, bowed his head and in a whisper said, "Master, if you cannot use me unless you cut me down, then do your will and cut."

"Bamboo," the master said, "I would cut off your leaves and branches and strip you naked." "Oh, Master, spare me," Bamboo begged. "Cut me down if you must, but do not lay my beauty in the dust." "Ah, Bamboo," the master said, "alas, I cannot use you unless I cut them away."

The Sun hid her face. The listening butterfly fearfully glided away. Bamboo shivered in terrible expectancy and whispered, "Master, cut away." "Bamboo," the master said, "I must divide you in two and cut out your heart, for if I do not, I cannot use you." "Master," Bamboo answered, "then cut me in two and divide, but use me."

And so the master of the garden took Bamboo and cut him down and hacked off his branches and stripped away his leaves and divided him in two and cut out his heart and lifted him gently and carried him where there was a spring of fresh, sparkling water in the midst of the master's dry fields. And putting Bamboo down, one end in the spring and the other in the channels to the dry fields, the master laid down his beloved Bamboo.

And the Spring sang a welcome. And the sparkling, clear water raced joyously down the channel of Bamboo's torn body into the dry fields. And rice was planted and the days went by. And the Wind came to pay a visit. And the Sun shone her face. And soon bright green, new shoots of life came forth and the harvest came. And in that day, Bamboo, once so glorious in the garden, gave life to many and was even yet more glorious in his brokenness. For in his brokenness, life became abundant. Through his brokenness, the master could give new life to the dry fields. And by his brokenness, many were made whole.

Even though this ancient oriental parable may have originally been intended to say little more than that bamboo is useful and to give praise to nature for its goodness, we know it has deeper meaning than that. And especially as we hear it this morning, we cannot help but understand that it is a parable about the sacrifice and suffering of Jesus. It is a picture of Christ and of you and me.

In the book of Philippians Saint Paul recognizes the same picture when he writes, "Have this mind among yourselves which is yours in Christ Jesus, who being in the form of God, did not count equality with God a thing to be grasped, but emptied himself and took on himself the form of a servant and was made human. And being found in human form, he humbled himself and became obedient unto death, even a death on the cross."

In his immortal work *Paradise Lost*, John Milton tells a story of an angel who sought to be equal with God. And for this the angel was cast out of heaven and reigned in hell. Milton reports this fallen angel as saying, "Better to reign in hell than to serve in heaven."

What a difference between those words and the words of Saint Paul! Christ is One who did not count equality with God as something important, but emptied himself to the level of humanity and in humility and obedience gave himself to death. It is an act of giving love, the supreme sacrifice of self for others.

As we gather today so near the cross, as we remember Jesus' triumphant entry into Jerusalem, his suffering and death, we cannot help but be humbled by his example. History records a time in the nineteenth century when Chancellor Bismarck of Prussia chose to make a grand entry into Jerusalem. He chose to do so then on a great white stallion, accompanied by so many officials and officers that a whole section of the wall that surrounds ancient Jerusalem had to be removed. A person of greatness enters a city that way, or so we think — with limousines and loudspeakers, press releases and secret service agents closing the streets. But not our Lord. He enters on a donkey!

For Jesus is different — not only in his manner of entrance — but also in the way he leaves. For as we hear in the reading today, he leaves on a cross. He humbles himself and is obedient to the Father. Just as Bamboo was stripped of his leaves, his stalk split in two, his heart cut out and laid down, so Christ lay aside his divine nature. Stripped of his dignity, forsaken of his friends, broken in body, he, too, is laid down on a cross.

In a *Peanuts* cartoon, Charlie Brown and Linus are standing next to each other, staring up at a star-filled sky. "Would you like to see a falling star, Linus?" Charlie Brown asks. "Sure ..." Linus replies, but then he hesitates. "Then again," he says, "I'd hate to think that it fell just on my account."

God came to us in Jesus. Like a lamb led to slaughter, he died on our account — with humility and with love. What devotion our God shows us! And the question that must be asked is: What response can we make for all this?

Saint Paul again has the answer for that. In the same chapter of Philippians he writes, "Therefore God has highly exalted him and bestowed upon him a name which is above all other names, that at the name of Jesus, every knee should bow and every tongue confess that Jesus Christ is Lord."

We need to join the crowds that welcomed Jesus as he entered Jerusalem. We need to join the chorus of children who sang his praise. We need to offer our lives to him in service and praise, to bow our knees and to use our tongues to give him praise, for he offered himself for us.

We used to call this Sunday Palm Sunday and so it is. But in recent years, our lectionary has instructed us to think of it more as "The Sunday of the Passion" and rightly so. For somehow today the triumph of his entry is diminished by our knowledge of the tragedy to follow. Somehow our shouts of praise are tempered by the cries of "crucify him!" that would echo in the streets later. Our voices may sing, "Hosanna," but our hearts want to cry out, "Turn back." Our worship may welcome him with praise, but part of us wants to say, "Get away from this place, Jesus! For only death awaits you here!"

And how often our Lord could have turned back! How many times the security of home and family must have tugged at his heart! After the experience in the wilderness, he could have turned back. It was clear then that the road he was to travel would lead to a cross. He could have turned back the many times he found himself with the disciples with little to eat and no place to call home. He could have turned back when the Pharisees hounded his every step, cross-examined his every gesture, stirred up public opinion against him, and with every passing moment plotted his death.

He could have turned back after announcing that one of the disciples would betray him or after all the disciples fell asleep in the Garden. He could have turned back when they turned their backs on him and ran. But he didn't. His heart would not let him.

For his heart was filled with love for the Master. His heart heard the cries of the poor, the bitter accusations of the abandoned, the dangling despair of those who were lost. His heart saw the faces — some wrinkled and weeping, some blank with boredom, obscured by fear or twisted with hate. He could have turned back when he saw the faces, but he didn't. Because among the faces that he saw were your face and mine, our fears and our tears, our hopes and our silent prayers. And it is for that reason that we offer him our worship and praise, that we seek to serve him and follow.

To be cut down and lifted up — that was his purpose. Jesus himself spoke of it to Nicodemus when he said, "Just as Moses lifted up the snake in the wilderness, so must the Son of Man be lifted up, that whoever believes in him may not perish but have eternal life." Cut down and lifted up for our salvation. Stripped naked of his beauty, and laid down that through him God's life might flow to us, our dry hearts might be nourished, and the seed of faith within us might grow and produce a harvest of righteousness. Cut down and lifted up — God's gift of grace for us and our hope of life eternal. Amen.

A New
Command

In his book *Life Looks Up*, Charles Templeton remarks how ironic it is that the course of human history has been affected so positively and negatively by events that have occurred in two small upper rooms. One of them is a drab flat in London's Westside, dirty, curtainless, with stacks of articles on the table and worn manuscripts, aborted attempts wadded up in the trash can. Seated at the table a man labors over a writing, a writing that would overthrow governments, enslave millions of people, and negatively affect the course of history for a generation to come. The man: Karl Marx; his writing: *Das Kapital*, the handbook for the Communist revolution.

But there's another upper room that also figures in the course of human history: this one located in one of the oldest cities of the world, Jerusalem, and here also there was a table. Thirteen gather at this table to share a meal and to hear the words of a man whose love and sacrifice would make a lasting impact on human history. His message — that faith in God and love for one another would revolutionize governments and change the lives of countless generations of people to come.

How strange it is that some 1800 years later, Karl Marx would proclaim that strife among people, rigid control of possessions, strict limitation of personal freedom and a move toward a godless

49

society would bring about the perfect world that humanity was seeking. For the key to the kind of life that you and I desire had already been given us. It was there in the words of Jesus in that upper room.

Hear the words that Jesus spoke to his disciples that evening as he gathered them together for the Last Supper. From the Gospel of John, Chapter 13, Jesus says:

> *A new command I give you: Love one another. As I have loved you, so you must love one another. By this all men will know that you are my disciples, if you love one another.*

This is my commandment: that you love one another as I have loved you. This is my will for you. This is what I expect. This is my desire for all people — that my joy may be in you and your joy may be full. Love one another. What a model for successful living!

When the play *Peter Pan* first premiered on the London stage in 1904, author Sir James Barrie began to hear complaints from parents who were upset with his play. They even got together and petitioned him to make a change in the script.

It seems that in the original version, Peter Pan told the Darling children that if they simply believed strongly enough, they could fly. And apparently there were children who had seen that play who tried to do just that, who took Peter Pan literally at his word, and hurt themselves attempting to fly. So without hesitation, Sir James altered the script to include the cautionary statement that children could fly, but only if they had first been sprinkled with "fairy dust." And because real fairy dust is in short supply, children were no longer in danger.

Such is the power of a positive example. Love one another *as I have loved you*, Jesus tells us. Let my love for you be an example; let my love for you inspire you, enrich, enlighten, and empower you to love one another. That same evening as the disciples gathered with Jesus for his final meal, Jesus demonstrated for them the meaning of love. Listen to what John says in his Gospel:

Jesus, knowing that the Father had given all things into
his hands, and that He had come from God and was going
to God, rose from supper, laid aside his garments, and
girded himself with a towel. Then he poured water into
a basin, and began to wash the disciples' feet, and to
wipe them with the towel.

He washed the disciples' feet. He took for himself the role of a
servant and washed their feet. And the disciples were horrified.
How could he, their leader, serve them? That's not the way it's
done. In the real world, we strive to be served by others. But not
when we follow the example of Jesus' love. Jesus says,

Do you know what I have done to you? You call me
Teacher and Lord; and you are right, for so I am. If I
then, your Lord and Teacher, have washed your feet, you
also ought to wash one another's feet. For I have given
you an example, that you should do as I have done to
you.

Love one another. Follow the example of my love as you serve
and care for one another. Pastor Roy L. Smith, who for many
years was the editor of *Guideposts* magazine, was not yet eighteen
years old when he received a hurried message at school that his
father had been hurt at the mill where he worked. As Roy ran
down Main Street of Nickerson, Kansas, a blunt man cried out to
him, "No use runnin', kid. He's already gone."

Roy's father was a skilled mechanic and flour miller and highly
respected in town. On the day of his funeral every business in
town was closed. The day before the funeral, Roy and his brother
went up to the mill to collect their father's things. Among the
tools and belongings were the clothes he had on the day he was
killed. They were all packed up in a paper sack and there on top of
the sack were his dad's shoes, soles turned up. And there in the
center of each shoe was a big hole in the sole.

The day Roy's dad died, he had stood on the concrete floor
with a hole in his shoes. Now that's not something that's so
remarkable for those who grew up years ago when times were

tough. What is remarkable, however, is the fact that less than a week before he died, his father had taken Roy down to the department store and bought him a new pair of shoes to wear to school. Looking back, Roy says that he would have given anything if only he had put a good pair of shoes on his father's feet for the last hour of his life.

That's the kind of love that God has for us in Christ Jesus. Love that sacrifices itself for us. Love that bends down in service and reaches out in love. This is my commandment: that you love one another as I have loved you. If we are to have Jesus as our role model, it means that we are going to have to roll up our sleeves and get down to the business of loving one another. It means that we are going to have to commit ourselves to serving Christ in the needs of those around us. As Jesus has said,

> *Whatever you do to the least of these, my brothers and sisters, you do unto me. Love one another, as I have loved you.*

At no time does a person speak with greater sincerity and honesty than when that person knows he is going to die. Those are times when foolishness has no room, when sincerity and truth have center stage. As Jesus gathered his disciples together with him in that upper room, he knew that the end was near. He knew that the cross awaited him. And he knew what his disciples needed to hear. That's why he left them that final commandment, that *Living Will* for them — that they love one another.

As we gather to receive his body and blood, as we gather to "do this in remembrance," we are to remember his Will for us — that we love one another. That night in the upper room Jesus knew what it would take to change the world — not strife and revolution, not warfare and bloodshed, but love, sincere, self-sacrificing love on the part of his people.

Last November, Dr. Avi Ben-Abraham, head resident of the American Cryogenics Society, told an audience in Washington, D.C., that several high-ranking Roman Catholic church leaders had privately told him that despite the church's public stance against research in genetics and gene reproduction and experimentation in artificial life production, they personally supported his way-out research. According to Ben-Abraham, those church leaders hope to reproduce Jesus Christ from DNA fibers found on the Shroud of Turin.

If Dr. Ben-Abraham is right, somebody better tell those venerable church leaders that Jesus has no desire to be cloned — except in the lives of those who love him and follow him. That's why he takes bread and wine and gives us himself in Holy Communion, to bring us forgiveness and to strengthen us to love one another. This is my will — this is my commandment for you. In Jesus' name. Amen.

The
Ultimate Mystery

Good Friday   *John 18:1—19:42*

An event is like a living organism. Its life depends on the inter-working of all of its parts. Take any one part and you steal the life from the whole thing. This is especially true of John's account of the death of Jesus. John, the theologian of the Gospel writers, more than any of the rest, views the crucifixion of Jesus as more than mere history. In the death of Jesus, John sees the person and purpose of Christ revealed. Let's take a step forward and, by means of John's description of Calvary, stand at the foot of the cross and meet this Christ.

The Gospel writer John tells us, "So the soldiers took charge of Jesus. Carrying his own cross, he went out to the place of the Skull (which in Aramaic is called Golgotha)." Evidently something about the site resembled a human skull. For those who have gone to Jerusalem and visited the "Garden Tomb" site, this description has meaning. There just outside the ancient city walls of Jerusalem at the site of an old stone quarry is a hill, and as one stands and looks at the rock face, on the side of the hill are two indentations and an outcropping that look like eye sockets and a nose. Perhaps it was this resemblance to a skull that gave the site its name.

But for John, more than a physical resemblance was intended. This place was called Golgotha because it was a place of death, a "skull" place, symbolic of human death and decay. The sign of a skull. A skull and crossbones. We use it to label poison. Pirates used it on their flags to signal their evil intent, their lack of mercy, and to inflict fear into the hearts of others. Here at Golgotha, the symbol was real. This was called "the place of the skull" not only because of the shape of the rock outcroppings. This was a place of death. Here Jesus would die.

John tells us that Jesus is led out "bearing his own cross." No mention is made by John of Jesus' falling and another being asked to take his place. For John it is important that Jesus walk the way of the cross alone, that he bear the instrument of his own sacrifice alone (just as Isaac in the Old Testament was to be sacrificed by his father, Abraham, so will Jesus be — only this time there will be no ram caught in the bushes to save him). Jesus must bear the cross alone and in doing so show us that he will also bear the sins of all humanity.

John goes on. Fastened to the cross was a sign which read: "Jesus of Nazareth, King of the Jews." It was there because Pilate had ordered it put there — not as a testimony of faith, but as a sign of his contempt of the Jews. They were so troublesome. Attempts to placate them only brought pronouncements that "God was their king, not Caesar." And so to poke fun at them, Pilate had that sign put there, proclaiming that Jesus was King of the Jews.

Next notice the soldiers, busy with their usual pastime, dividing the spoils. We even say it, don't we? "To the victor belong the spoils." However, in this case there was little to fight over: some garments, little better than rags, and a robe, for which the soldiers cast lots. But in so doing, the soldiers became part of the Scripture's fulfillment, for in Psalm 22, the Psalmist speaks of the Messiah to come, whose hands and feet will be pierced, and whose garments are divided and robe given to the victor.

The One spoken of was Jesus — the One whom God would send to bear the burden of humanity and our sinfulness. This is the One who is pierced. This is the lamb sacrificed, the fulfillment of promise, and the gift of salvation.

Finally our survey of the scene at Calvary must include Jesus and those nearby. We see a group of women and a single apostle, gathered at his feet. They gathered there as do families around the bed of a dying loved one. They gathered there to share their pain and lean on one another, so their sorrow and anguish would not overcome them. There they stand. There in the midst of the anger and hatred of the crowd, the mocking of the onlookers, the scorn of the priests and the insult of the soldiers. There, in that place of shame outside the City of Kings, Jerusalem, there they stand waiting for it to be over.

In the midst of those at the foot of the cross is his mother, Mary. What must be going through her mind? Perhaps only a parent who has lost a child to death can truly know. Perhaps only those who have experienced the death of a loved one can truly describe the emotions. Is she thinking of the angels singing and the shepherds at his birth? You know, it's not very far from Bethlehem to Calvary. The distance is really not more than five miles. You could walk it in a couple hours, probably less time than it took for it to be over that fateful Friday. The journey of a lifetime over in the span of a few hours. Perhaps she recalls the words of wise old Simeon at the Temple when Jesus was only a few days old. Simeon had told her, "This child is meant for the rising and fall of many and a sword will pierce your soul also." Maybe it is his own words that she thinks of, the works of wonder, the miracles of God, and the kindness he showed. Or perhaps she remembers the times he spoke of his own death.

What was on her mind we shall never know. Nevertheless, Jesus now speaks to her and even in his hour of greatest need, he thinks of her, provides for her, and assures her that she will be cared for by the disciple who stands nearby.

Events now rush to their conclusion. John writes for us, "Jesus, knowing that all was now finished, said, 'I thirst.' " He knew what was happening. This was no surprise to him. He knew he was dying, and he also knew the Scripture, and so to fulfill the Scripture, he said, "It is finished." It is accomplished. It is done. And having done that, he bowed his head and died. Having done all that the Father had requested of him, he offered up his spirit. And with those words, the Gospel writer John concludes his description of the events that fateful Friday. Note, my friends, that I say description and not explanation.

For no matter how skillfully John may write about the happenings that day, he cannot explain the event. For he cannot bring reason to this event — because the cross is not reasonable. In one sense, we can approach it logically (as we have done in this sermon today). We can describe what happened, reason from one position to another, and formulate doctrines regarding it as theologians have done throughout the centuries.

But no matter how hard we try, we cannot fully explain the cross and Jesus' death. For it will always remain a mystery. This is a riddle that only God can solve. Think of it! The cross, an instrument of torture so cruel that Rome forbad its use on a Roman citizen. A mob of people condemning the innocent, choosing instead to release a common criminal. And the Son of God in the hands of sinful men! No, the cross is a mystery and, try as we may, we cannot impose reason upon it. That the Creator would allow himself to die for God's sinful creation! That the Son of God should suffer so! Centuries ago, the famous church leader Saint Anselm wrote a young man who had his doubts and misgivings about the cross, saying, "Son, you have yet to consider the seriousness of sin."

And that is it. Until we consider the seriousness of our sinfulness, unless we recognize in the horror of the cross our failure before God, our own shortcoming to live as God wishes that we live, we cannot understand the cross. For the cross confronts us with our sinfulness. Here at the cross is revealed the whole vile catalog of sins. Every wrong appetite, every evil desire, every wrong action or unwholesome thought is brought together there that day. James Russell Lowell tells of a painting in Brussels in which God is about to create the world and an angel is depicted as attempting to hold back the arm of God as if to say, "If about to create such a world, stay Thy Hand." But that is not the answer.

It would be easy to blame all this on God, but we cannot. God did not create this world filled with crime, violence, and death that we have come to know. God did not intend for people and their governments to be at war with each other. God did not think up schemes of greed and corruption that would take the savings of the poor and elderly and spend it for penthouses, chauffeurs, and parties. God did not establish an economic system where, even in the wealthiest country of the world, the poor cannot afford homes to live in.

No, this is not God's doing. It is our own. We cannot blame God for the cross. The guilt is ours. And yet the mystery of the cross is just that. This is God's cross. In God's Son, Jesus, God has chosen to bear the cross, to take the punishment that is rightly ours and make it God's own. And therein lies the ultimate mystery of the cross — the mystery of God's love for us. For the cross is most of all the message of God's love, of God's eternal forgiveness, of God's grace at work, pouring itself down for you and me.

For the cross is God calling a sinful and wandering humanity back to himself. It is God offering comfort to Peter who denied Jesus. It is God offering forgiveness to Paul who persecuted Christ's followers, acceptance to Mary Magdalene whose sinful life mocked God, and God's love to you and me.

In Stroudsburg, Pennsylvania, there is a tomb to an unknown Union soldier who died fighting in the Civil War. When President Abraham Lincoln heard of it, he had the tomb inscribed, "Abraham Lincoln's Substitute. He died that I might live." And so we might inscribe the cross. "He died that we might live."

As we stand at the foot of the cross today, we see the depth of our sinfulness and yet even more wonderfully, the extent of God's love for us. We see the power of God's forgiveness and the grace to begin again. It is a promise that we who are God's children have in God and in God alone, the kingdom and the power and the glory, forever and ever. Amen.

In Jesus' name. Amen.

Taking The Risk
Out Of Dy(e)ing

Easter Sunday   *John 20:1-18*

Not long ago a newspaper carried an unusual headline. It read, "Test Takes Risk Out of Dyeing." Now, obviously, it was talking about dyeing hair. An expert was being quoted as saying that before dyeing your hair, you should test one strand to see how it works. Now that seems to make good sense to me. But it was the headline which attracted my attention: "Test Takes Risk Out of Dyeing."

Another recent news article intrigued me even more. It was a report that archaeologists in the Holy Land had uncovered the tomb of the High Priest Caiaphas. It was Caiaphas, you remember, who presided over the plot to have Jesus arrested, convicted, and crucified. Do you know what they found when they opened his tomb? They found Caiaphas, or I should say, they found the decayed bones of the man who instigated Jesus' death.

I could not help but be struck by the fact that archaeologists found the high priest's decayed body in the tomb — but nobody has ever found the body of Jesus. Why? Well, you and I know, don't we?

Remember what happened? Journey back with me for a moment to that first Easter morning. While it is still dark, through the deserted streets of Jerusalem, three men run along, hurrying to the residence of the High Priest Caiaphas. In the courtyard, a guard stops them. "See Caiaphas now? Impossible! You'll have to wait until dawn at least!" Later, after the sun has risen, Caiaphas meets with the three soldiers, and hears the incredible news that the tomb they were charged to guard is empty.

Caiaphas at first is puzzled, then angry, then thoughtful, for the men have no explanation. Repeated questioning will not shake their story. No, they had not fallen asleep. There had been some strange stirring in the garden, an earthquake had shaken the ground, the stone was dislodged, and the tomb was empty.

And so Caiaphas, the consummate politician, came up with an idea. The Scriptures tell us, "When the chief priest had met with the elders and devised a plan, they met with the soldiers and gave them a large sum of money, telling them, 'Say that his disciples came during the night and stole him away while you were asleep.' "

But nothing could have been further from the truth. For while this whole charade was going on, the despair and disillusionment of the disciples were almost complete. Take Simon Peter for instance. His heart was filled with despair over his own shameful denial of Jesus, and his mind was clouded with disillusionment over the fate of Jesus. The One in whom they had placed their hopes was now dead. All chances were gone.

And so Peter says, "I'm going fishing." What else is there to do? Life has to go on, and perhaps they can pick up the pieces where they were dropped when Jesus came along and called them from their nets to follow him.

Perhaps they could get away. Perhaps they could forget. Maybe the sting of the sea wind on their faces, the rough nets sliding through their fingers, the tug of the fish could help them forget — forget that certain face, that voice, that smile. Perhaps they could start again.

The women, too, were dealing with their grief the only way they knew how. They had watched as his dead body had been lowered from the cross, hastily anointed, and placed in the borrowed tomb of Joseph of Arimathea. And so now, on that first Easter morning, they made their way to the tomb. But as they walked to the tomb, they were preoccupied with one problem: "Who will roll aside the stone, that we may go in?" They did not go to greet a risen Savior, but to complete their duty toward a dead man.

The women had no grandiose plan to deceive humanity for centuries to come. They had been there at Calvary. They had seen him die. And now all they wanted was to complete the final acts of love and respect for their dead leader.

We can't blame them for their reaction that Easter morning, can we? You know what they did. They ran for their lives! Time and time again in the Scriptures, the announcement of the resurrection is preceded by the words, "Do not be afraid." The angel who greeted the women at the tomb said that. "Do not be afraid. You are looking for Jesus of Nazareth who was crucified. See the place where he lay? He is not here. He has risen. Go and tell the disciples."

Mary Magdalene, unable to understand, unable to bear the pain, so filled with grief and despair that she could not even run, returns to the garden and meets a man there who asks her, "Woman, why are you weeping?" "Because they have taken my lord away," she says. And then the voice of the One who holds life and death in his very hands, the One who had forgiven and restored her, makes himself known to her — with just one word — as he says her name, "Mary."

And just as suddenly as the new day dawns, Mary understood. She knew. She knew then that life is no brief candle that flickers and goes out. That by the power of God Almighty, Christ had risen, and brings with him the promise of life everlasting. That for all who turn to him in faith, that same light of a new day, the light of Easter, will dawn, bright and glorious.

For that is the message of Easter — that in the resurrection of Jesus a new day dawns for all of us. How many have stood or dreaded standing where those faithful women stood before the dawn of Easter morning — there in the valley of the shadow of death? How many have experienced the fear and dread that is ours when tragedy occurs or sickness comes calling or a loved one or someone near us dies?

It is then that we need to hear the words of the angels, "Do not be afraid. He has risen!" That's the message of Easter. It says:

"Stop! Stop and listen. Stand still long enough in the presence of God to hear God calling your name." That's what Mary did.

Stop. Not when death trips you up or the grave stands in your way, and certainly not before you reach the empty tomb of Jesus. Stop and hear Jesus call your name. Remember the words we speak at baptism, saying, "Child of God, you have been sealed by the Holy Spirit and marked with the cross of Christ forever." Stop and hear God calling you.

Hear the words the Gospel writer Luke records the angels saying as they ask, "Why do you seek the Living God among dead things?" Why do you return to places of death? Why go back to sin and wrongdoing? Why go back to habits of life that bring pain and heartache to you and those around you?

Stop and hear God speak to you today. Hear God call you forth from places of darkness and death into the light of the resurrection. Let Easter dawn upon you. Let the resurrection fill you with faith and hope and obedience to the voice of God.

Perhaps you noticed the humorous little news item in *Newsweek* last March. It was a letter written from the Greenville County, South Carolina, Department of Social Services to a dead person. The letter said, "Your food stamps will be stopped effective immediately because we have received notice that you passed away. Thank you for your attention to this matter. You may reapply if there is any change in your circumstances."

I don't know about you, but there is only one person I know of who has ever had that kind of "change of circumstance" and that is Jesus Christ our Lord. He lives and because he lives, we also may live eternally. As Mary Magdalene stood in the garden and heard Jesus call her name, she made a discovery that would change her life forever. She knew then that God was in control and that Jesus lives forever. She knew then that God was with her and that no matter what road she would travel from then on God would accompany her.

And that is the gift of Easter. The gift that God longs to give you and me. The promise — the assurance — of God's love and care for us. The promise that as Christ is resurrected from the grave, so you and I may experience new life in him.

There is a terrible story about a man whose wife had a cat that he despised. That cat was always under his feet, always tearing up the furniture, leaving cat hair all over. Finally, one weekend when his wife was away, the man took the cat out and drowned it. When his wife returned, she was in hysterics when she couldn't find the cat. So to comfort her, he took out an ad in the newspaper and offered a $1,000 reward for anyone finding the cat. A friend, hearing about the man's offer, said, "Man, you have to be crazy. $1,000 for that cat and you didn't even like it!" The man just smiled and replied, "When you know what I know, you can afford to take the risk."

Dear friends, there is only one way I know to take the risk out of living and dying. And that is to know what you and I know. To trust in God and to live out our faith. The headline this morning should read, "Christ Takes the Risk Out of Dying." Caiaphas' bones lie in his tomb, as do all those who elevate themselves above Christ. For God is in control. Death is defeated. He is risen! Alleluia! Amen.

Do Not Be Doubting
But Believe!

Easter 2   *John 20:19-31*

What a week it had been for the disciples. Everything had happened so fast! One moment the crowd welcomed Jesus into Jerusalem with shouts of hosanna, palm branches, and a hero's welcome. And then suddenly, a couple of days later, he was arrested, taken to the cross and crucified. The disciples must have been shell-shocked. They had been taken to the heights of joy and expectancy, only to have their hopes and dreams crushed with Jesus' death. It's no wonder that they hid out. They were afraid. They thought they were next. If Jesus could be killed in such a cruel and unfair manner, what about them? So it's no wonder that they gathered behind locked doors. It's no wonder they doubted the news of Jesus' resurrection.

And what a day it had been! It began with Mary first. She had gone to the tomb early in the morning and found it empty. Peter and one of the other disciples went racing to the garden. They returned with mixed reports. Later Mary came and told them that she had spoken with Jesus.

Imagine her excitement, the quickened pulse, and the rapid speech as she tried to share the news with the disciples. But we can also imagine the difficulty they had in believing it. For it is incredible news! The One who was dead is now alive. On the face of it, it is impossible. In fact, the Bible tells us that their first response to the story was to regard it as idle nonsense, told by a distraught and hysterical woman.

That very evening the disciples gathered again, once more behind locked doors, not knowing for sure what to think about what had happened that first Easter day. And in the middle of their confusion, Jesus came and stood among them. His words to them are his words for us. He said to the disciples, "Peace be with you." Just when things seem terrible, Jesus is there. Just when things seem hopeless, Jesus is present. Just when things seem impossible, Jesus can help.

For the disciples, things could not have gotten worse. By the end of that first Easter weekend, just about everything in their lives was in shambles. Their careers had been abandoned. (I don't know if the disciples thought in those terms. I rather suspect that the idea of career is a twentieth century concept — but nonetheless they must have reflected on what they would do for a living next!) Three years before they had heard Jesus say to them, "Follow me," and had cast their lots with him. Following Jesus was to have been their future. And now all that was gone. Their futures were in shambles. What would they do now? For Jesus was gone — no, worse than gone — he had been crucified. And perhaps the same fate awaited them. Was there any future for any of them after what had just happened? Their faith was shaken. They had trusted Jesus. They had believed in him. Their whole understanding of God, everything they believed and lived for had died with him — just collapsed, like a house of cards! And it was all gone!

For the disciples, just when everything seemed at its worst, Jesus was there for them. Standing in the midst of them. Alive. There to grant them strength and hope. And that would make the difference for them. In fact, they would go to their graves, these disciples, almost all of them to hostile, martyr's graves, not the "Now I lay me down to sleep" variety, but the kind of graves that we pray never comes to us or our loved ones ... those disciples would go to their graves confident that even when things get *that* terrible, Jesus Christ was there and that was all that mattered for them.

That is what happened to those disciples that night behind locked doors. Jesus came to them and changed their lives. Jesus came in the midst of them and they emerged as different people, confident and assured of God's love for them.

So we can understand the way Thomas must have felt. He hadn't been there. He had missed out. For him, the darkness of night still filled his heart. For him, life was still hopeless. His hopes had died with Jesus. For him, the future was still unsure. For he had yet to meet the Risen Lord, and because of that, doubt filled his heart.

"Unless I see for myself, I will not believe. Unless I can feel the marks of the nails with my own fingers and touch the wound in his side with my own hands, I will not believe." Can you sense Thomas' misery? Can you hear his loneliness, his separation and pain? I think you can, because we have all felt it. We have all gone through the same experience. We have trusted and been hurt. We have loved and lost. We have reached out in reconciliation to others, only to have them reject us and snap back in pain. We have all been where Thomas was — hurt and afraid to trust again. We understand Thomas. He will be careful now. He will be slow to believe and reluctant to trust. As for Thomas, he must see for himself.

We know all about doubt, don't we? For we have all felt the same way Thomas did. Dave Dravecky, former pitcher for the San Francisco Giants, lost his arm to cancer a few years ago. It was a devastating experience. It is bad enough to have cancer, let alone to face the amputation of an arm. And then on top of that, to lose a promising career as a major league baseball player. Naturally Dave was filled with many questions.

During his time of struggle, he began to receive letters from people all over the country, people who had learned of his illness. Most of those letters were letters of encouragement. Some people wrote him looking for answers. They knew he had been through so much and yet had been able to keep his faith, and they wanted to know how he had done it. One day he received the following letter:

Dear Mr. Dravecky, If there is a God who cares so much about you, why did he allow you to have the surgery in the first place? I have lived 41 years in this old world and have yet to see any piece of genuine evidence that there is anything real about any of those religious beliefs you talk about. God certainly does not love me and has never done a single thing to express that love for me. I have had to fight for everything I ever got in life. Nobody cares about what happens to me and I don't care about anybody else either. Can't you see the truth that religion is nothing more than a crutch used by a lot of weaklings who can't face reality and that the church is nothing but a bunch of hypocrites who care nothing for each other and whose faith extends not to their actions or daily lives but is only just a bunch of empty phrases spouted off to impress others?

A cruel letter, isn't it? How would you have responded to it? Dave Dravecky received it after he had seen his baseball career taken from him and lost his arm. He wrote the man back. He told the letter writer that he knew how he felt because he had faced the same doubts. He too had wondered if God had abandoned him. He too had questioned if anyone cared. He too wondered if his faith were not just empty words. But when things seemed the worst, Jesus was there. "I am convinced," Dravecky wrote, "that there is a God. That no matter what happens to me, there is a purpose for it and behind that purpose stands a loving, caring God." The same God who came to the disciples. The same Resurrected Jesus who stood among them and said, "Peace be with you."

It was the peace that Dave Dravecky had experienced which enabled him to face his loss with grace and faith. And it was precisely the same peace that the man who wrote that cruel letter has never found — peace with God or even peace with himself. For when doubt dominates our lives, that is precisely what we lose, peace with God and peace with ourselves.

Thomas knew that. He knew what it was like to live without peace. He had experienced it for a whole week. That's what the Gospel reading is about this morning — a week of darkness, a week spent without hope, a week without Jesus.

When Thomas refused to believe, it was not just the other disciples' word that he doubted. It was life itself that he rejected. It was a rejection of hope, a refusal to believe that life can have meaning, that life goes on even after death. We can hear that so very clearly in the cruel letter Dravecky received, can't we? The story of Thomas shows us that there is no hope without the resurrection of Jesus. There is no way to make sense of our earthly existence without God. But then that shouldn't be a surprise to us. The Gospel writer John said that when he wrote, "He who believes in the Risen Christ has life. And he who does not believe is dead already." Dead already! Those are his words. "He who does not believe is dead already."

When we allow doubt to dominate our lives, when we close ourselves off to the possibilities of God, when we live our lives with only death as the end for us, we walk through life down a dead-end road. But doubt need not lead to death. Doubt does not have to destroy faith. Listen to what Jesus said to Thomas when on the week following Easter he appeared to him. In verse 26 it says, "A week later his disciples were again in the house, and Thomas was with them. Although the doors were shut, Jesus came and stood among them and said, 'Peace be with you.' Then he said to Thomas, 'Put your finger here and see my hands. Reach out your hand and put it in my side. **Do not doubt but believe.**' "

There is a remedy to doubt. There is help for us when we find ourselves filled with questionings and doubt, when the world seems to collapse in upon us and all our props are knocked away. Take Thomas as an example. Thomas made the mistake we often make. He thought he could go it alone. Devastated by the death of Jesus, he separated himself from the other disciples. "Give me some room," he said. "I just have to work this out alone." He sought solitude in his pain, isolation for his loneliness, and thought he could maintain his trust in God all alone. But what we see is that his doubts came from being absent from the disciples, from being separate and alone when Jesus appeared to them on the first Easter day.

But his doubts were answered in the presence of the other disciples. It was only in the fellowship of believers, only through the Body of Christ, that Thomas found the assurance that he so deperately sought and needed. "Put your finger here," Jesus said to him. "See my hands. Reach out your hand and touch me, if you must. Do not be doubting but believe."

When doubt dominates our lives, when doubt draws us apart from the church, then doubt can be deadly. But when doubt leads us to look deeper for God, when doubt sends us searching for God's wisdom and goodness, when doubt forces us more fully into the fellowship of believers, then even doubt can be a blessing for us just as it was for Thomas. For in the midst of doubt, Jesus is there. Even when things seem darkest, a light shines: Jesus, who said, "I am the light of the world."

On July 4, 1952, Florence Chadwick made an attempt to swim the channel between Catalina Island and the California coast. Unfortunately, it was a fog-filled day. She entered the cold water, swimming for fifteen hours, fighting the cold, sharks and fog. Finally, she asked to be taken into the boat. Her assistants in the boat encouraged her to keep going for surely they must be close. But because she could not see land, only fog, she quit. After she got into the boat, they discovered that they were less than 500 meters from Catalina Island. Two months later, on a clear day, she tried again. This time, encouraged by the sun and fine weather, she met her goal. Only eleven hours and 27 minutes later, Florence Chadwick became the first woman to swim across the San Pedro Bay to Catalina Island.

When doubts and questionings cloud our vision, when troubles and difficulties close our eyes to the goodness of God, we need to move closer to our Savior. We need to draw more deeply into worship, spend more time in Scripture reading and prayer, and reach out more strongly to our brothers and sisters in the faith.

Mature faith, faith that serves us for a lifetime, is not a faith that has never experienced doubts. Rather it is faith that constantly searches and seeks, faith always on the lookout for Jesus, faith that trusts that even when the worst has happened, there in the middle of it stands Jesus. Jesus knew that was the kind of faith we need. That's why he said, "Peace be with you. Do not be doubting, but believe. Blessed are those who have not seen and yet believe." That's his promise for us — blessed are you and I, for in believing we have life in his name. Amen.

Real Solutions
To Real Problems

Easter 3   *John 21:1-19*

There's a story of a man who went to his doctor complaining about terrible neck pains, throbbing headaches, and recurring dizzy spells. The doctor examined him carefully and pronounced, "I'm sorry but I have bad news for you. The diagnosis is not good. But from what I can tell, you must have an unspecified brain tumor causing the problem. Unfortunately there is nothing we can do for you. It seems that you have only six months to live."

The doomed man left the doctor's office shaken and crushed, but he vowed that he would live his life to the fullest in the six months that he had left. Subsequently he went out and quit his job, cashed in his savings, and bought a new sports car, a closet full of new suits and expensive shoes. Then he went to an exclusive men's shop to buy a supply of the best quality tailored shirts available. He entered the shop and had the tailor measure him. As the tailor took the man's neck size, the dying man noticed him write down "size 16, neck."

"Wait a minute," the man said. "I don't wear a 16. I've always worn a size 14 shirt, and that's what I want now." "But if you wear a size 14," the tailor said, "you're apt to experience terrible neck pains, throbbing headaches, and recurring dizzy spells."

Without knowing it the tailor had unmasked the man's real problem. And that's the title for the sermon this morning — Real Solutions To Real Problems.

In some ways, this last chapter of John's gospel presents us with a problem. As we read it, it strikes us as strange. It's almost as if the evangelist John has concluded his gospel before writing the last chapter. At the end of chapter 20, he writes that his gospel has shown by the signs and wonders that "Jesus is the Christ, the Son of God, and that believing (we) may have life in his name." As we read those words, it is clear that here, in effect, John lays aside his pen and closes the book. But suddenly he remembers more. He realizes that the story is not yet finished. And so once again he takes up his pen and writes the final chapter. It's as if he remembers some final details, some loose ends that need tying up, some problems without clear solutions.

So he picks up his pen to write an epilogue — Chapter 21. He begins that epilogue with Peter and six of the other disciples. Remember — John has already told the story of Jesus' resurrection. He has already shared with his readers the appearance of Jesus to Mary and the disciples and to Thomas. But to tell the story of those resurrection appearances is not enough. There is more!

And so in today's Gospel reading, John tells another story — this time the story of Jesus' appearance to Peter and some other disciples, this time not in Jerusalem, not in Bethany, not some place where Jesus has been — but home, back home with the disciples. Back home fishing. And in doing so, it is almost as if John wants to remind us of something we might overlook elsewhere.

It is an interesting story, is it not? It is a story we can well identify with, especially this third Sunday after Easter. It is a "back to usual" story. It is a "fella's got to make a living" kind of story. Look at Peter and those disciples. They might as well have been twentieth century Christians by the way they acted, by their response to Easter, as quickly as things returned to normal in their lives. Having walked with Jesus, having heard his words and witnessed his miracles, having experienced the grief of the cross and the exhilaration of the resurrection, what do the disciples do? They go back to their boats. It is almost as if the past three years had not happened, as if it had all been a dream.

I told you a while ago that the theme for the sermon this morning was "Real Solutions To Real Problems," and that is what this story is about. However, as we look at the way the disciples acted after the resurrecton, you may be wondering. For the disciples it appeared as if the resurrection had made no difference in their lives. It's back to normal. Fishing can be good therapy, but it can also be lousy! Catching fish is one thing, but when the fish are not biting, there is plenty of time to think. And try as we might, it is often impossible to set our minds off of troubling events. It's like trying to keep your tongue from finding its way to the empty space left where you've lost a tooth.

It's not hard to imagine Peter's thoughts, is it? They must have gone back to the upper room and Jesus' words of warning that Peter would deny him; back to the Garden and the disciples' weariness and failure to watch with Jesus; back to the fire in the courtyard and his own unforgivable moments of denial. Why wouldn't Peter want to start over? Why wouldn't he want to get back to the boats and forget what had happened?

And that's why this morning's Gospel story is so important — for Peter and for each one of us. This morning's story is for all who have ever wished they could go back and start again, for everyone who has wondered what life would be like without God's forgiveness, without Easter and God's love. The story shows us what life would be like with only its idleness and self-directed busyness, its vanity and vulgarity, its failures and successes. The disciples show us that life without Easter adds up to futility.

Someone once said that half the mental health admissions each year would be unnecessary if the persons could only believe in the reality of Easter, if they could experience and believe in God's forgiveness and trust in the words of the resurrected Christ when he says, "I am with you always." These are words of promise not only for the troubled and guilt ridden, but also for the successful and self-consumed. Words for everyone who has ever experienced the truth and meaning of the words, "That night, they caught nothing." In the end when all was said and done, it added up to nothing.

Real solutions to real problems — that's the message this morning. Real solutions for real people — people like Saint Paul on the road to Damascus, his life consumed with hatred and directed at persecuting the new Christian church until he met Christ and his life was changed. People like Peter in the boat, his heart filled with hurt and weighed down by his own failure until he met Christ on the shore and experienced forgiveness.

The story this morning reminds us that after the resurrection nothing can ever be the same. Peter and the disciples may try to return to their boats, but they cannot for they have become fishers of *men*. They may go back to the same place. But they are not the same people. For the resurrection has changed them. Three years with the Master has changed their lives. Too many cripples walked. Too many graves were made open. Too many hours were spent listening to his Word and witnessing his power. Oh, this may be the same lake, the same boats, the same failure to catch fish, but these are not the same people. The resurrection has changed them. Nothing can ever be the same.

And perhaps that's what John wanted to tell us when he wrote the last chapter of his gospel. After the resurrection nothing can ever be the same. That's why Jesus appears to Peter and the disciples again — to remind them of that. It is God's grace for sinners, God's forgiveness for the fallen, and God's love for you and me. There on the shore of the Lake of Galilee we see how God treats us — with love and respect, with kindness and forgiveness. For just as Jesus stood on the shore and called to Peter, so he stands near us and calls to us as well. For his promise to us is the same. "Lo, I am with you always."

Did you ever wonder about these resurrection appearances of Jesus — how he keeps popping in and out of the disciples' lives? Here one moment and gone the next. It began the first evening of Easter and continues in the story today. What is the message he wants us to know? Could this be Jesus' way of underlining the words of his promise — "Lo, I am with you always"? There each moment they needed him most. There with the disciples in the grief and sadness as they gathered in the upper room. There with Thomas in his time of doubt. And now here today with Peter when his heart was filled with regret. It's almost as if Jesus is trying to demonstrate to the disciples the truth of his Word that he is near them always. Always ready to come in time of need. Moving in and out of their lives so naturally that soon they would come to expect him with them always.

An old man became gravely ill, and when the pastor came to visit, the pastor noticed a chair beside the man's bed. "Oh, goodness," the pastor said, "you've already had a visitor today." "Oh, no," the man replied, "let me tell you about that chair. Years ago, I told a friend that when I prayed at night, I frequently fell asleep right in the middle of my prayers. And my friend suggested that I put a chair beside my bed and imagine that Jesus is sitting there with me, because after all, he really is. So I started doing that, and you know what? It really helped. Sometimes I can even sense him sitting there beside me."

After talking with the man a while longer, the pastor went home and later that night he got a call from the man's daughter. She said, "Pastor, my dad just died. Can you come over?" So the pastor went to see her. The daughter said, "You know I was in the room and everything was fine. He wasn't struggling or anything. He was just lying there peacefully. So I left the room for a moment. When I came back, he had passed away. But what's strange is that when I came back in the room, I noticed that the chair was pulled back up beside his bed. Somehow he had managed to roll over on his side and stretch out his arm to the chair beside him."

Real solutions to real problems — that's what the resurrection of Jesus can mean to us. God's power and love flowing into our lives. The forgiveness and newness that can be ours in Jesus. The assurance of his presence with us always. Jesus calls to us today to drop down our nets and receive his blessing, to trust in his Word for us and to live in his presence. The same peace and contentment, the same joy and dedication that filled the disciples' lives can be ours. For the same Christ stands near us and speaks the same promise, "Lo, I am with you always." In Jesus' name. Amen.

God Is
Greater

Easter 4   *John 10:22-30*

Numbers. Our lives are filled with numbers. Each year we file our income taxes. Now that's an exercise in numbers to end all numbers games. Pages upon pages of numbers. And when it is finally prepared, we send it off to the Internal Revenue Service with our Social Security number on it. And the IRS takes all those numbers and puts them into a computer, along with the numbers of thousands and thousands of other people. And to them, we become a number.

The government knows us by our tax number. The state knows us by our driver's license number. The bank knows us by our account number. And when we retire, we'll be known by our Social Security number. And it goes on and on. In fact, sometimes I wonder if anybody knows us at all without a number!

And that's why this morning's Gospel reading is so significant, because it tells us that God knows us. He knows us intimately, in fact, better than we know ourselves. And that's important to remember. In spite of the fact that the image of sheep and shepherd is foreign to our experience, the words of the Gospel this morning hearken for us a truth that our human hearts long to hear. The Old Testament writer put it even more clearly when he wrote, "The Lord is my Shepherd, I shall not want." Jesus says it this morning,

"My sheep hear my voice and I know them and they follow me, and I give them eternal life."

A new kind of plane was on its first flight. It was full of reporters and journalists. A little while after takeoff, the captain's voice was heard over the speakers. "Ladies and gentlemen, I'm delighted to be your pilot for this plane's historic first flight. I can tell you the flight is going well. Nevertheless, I have to tell you about a minor inconvenience that has occurred. The passengers on the right side can, if they look out their window, see that the closest engine is slightly vibrating. That shouldn't worry you, because this plane is equipped with four engines and we are flying along smoothly at an acceptable altitude. As long as you are looking out the right side, you might as well look at the other engine on that side. You will notice that it is glowing, or more precisely one should say, burning. That shouldn't worry you either, since this plane is designed to fly with just two engines if necessary, and we are maintaining an acceptable altitude and speed. As long as we are looking out the plane, those of you on the left side shouldn't worry if you look out your side of the plane and notice that one engine that is supposed to be there is missing. It fell off about ten minutes ago. Let me tell you that we are amazed that the plane is doing so well without it. However, I will call your attention to something a little more serious. Along the center aisle all the way down the plane a crack has appeared. Some of you are, I suppose, able to look through the crack and may even notice the waves of the Atlantic Ocean below. In fact, those of you with very good eyesight may be able to notice a small lifeboat that was thrown from the plane. Well, ladies and gentlemen, you will be happy to know that your captain is keeping an eye on the progress of the plane from that lifeboat below."

Now, I realize that there are some situations that we ought not joke about, and a plane crash is perhaps one of them. But that little story about the plane and its pilot seemed so descriptive of our lives and the world today that I couldn't help but tell it. Sometimes we find ourselves in situations very similar to that plane flight. Everything around us seems to be falling apart and the person in charge seems to be as remote as the captain in the raft on the ocean far below.

But the good news this morning is that we are known by God and loved by God. And when God knows us and loves us, God will not abandon us. In spite of the senseless violence that seems so much a part of our world today, the innocent suffering and death that occur, our failures and our encounters with suffering, God wants us to know that God cares about us. God want us to know that God loves us with an everlasting love that calls us by name.

That's precisely the promise that God made with us from the beginning of time and that Jesus makes with us today. "I know my own and my own know me." We are more than just a number. In the midst of an uncertain world, faced with unknown dangers and threatened by unpredictable events of evil and violence around us, we are known by God and loved by God. "Even the hairs of your head are numbered," Jesus once said. For God is greater than anything that can threaten us in life. The death and resurrection of Jesus assure us of that, and the words of Jesus remind us of that once again today.

We need that reminder for there are all kinds of things in life that can threaten us. Accidents happen. Disasters come our way. Sickness strikes and disease often stalks us. No one knows when or where the next terrorist bomb may go off. We know that danger and death are part of our lives.

But the good news for us this morning is that whatever happens to us is not nearly as important as what happens in us. For God is greater than any danger. That's why these words of Jesus mean so much to us when he says, "I am the Good Shepherd. My sheep hear my voice and I know them and they follow me and I give them eternal life."

Many years ago the great preacher Harry Emerson Fosdick told of a teenage girl stricken with polio. As he visited with her, she told him about a conversation she'd had with one of her friends, who told her, "Affliction does so color life." To which this courageous young girl agreed, but said that she would choose which color. At her young age she had already discovered one of life's great secrets: It's not what happens to you that matters as much as what happens *in* you. For faith in God does not so much shield us from danger and death as it gives us the power to overcome it.

The great Christian devotional writer Corrie ten Boom nearly died during World War II in a Nazi prison camp. In one of her writings she recounts a conversation that she had. One day another prisoner asked her why God would let them suffer so much if God truly were a loving and caring God. Corrie replied, "There are many things I do not understand and cannot explain to you, but if you knew the Lord the way I know him, you wouldn't ask why. You'd be satisfied to know that God is good and that God loves us." Corrie knew that God was greater even than the evil that surrounded them in that concentration camp, and because God was greater, somehow God would see them through.

One of my favorite stories in the New Testament is the time when Jesus and the disciples were caught in a fishing boat on the Sea of Galilee when a storm came up. Do you remember how the disciples reacted when the waves and wind threatened their boat? The boat was rocking and it was slowly filling with water. It was beginning to sink and would soon dump them all into the sea. Through all this Jesus was asleep in the back of the boat. Finally the disciples woke the Master and hit him with a harsh question. "Master," they said, "Do you not care that we are about to perish?"

You and I have been with those disciples. We have seen the storm clouds rise and we have felt the wind howl and had the waves beat down upon us. It may be the death of a loved one. It may be a battle with disease or a fight with cancer. It could be a broken relationship or a time when your child didn't come home on time and worries overcame you. We have all been there and we have all shared the disciples' question, "Master, don't you care?"

And that's why the Gospel reading this morning is so precious to us. For Jesus' own words remind us that he does indeed care. "I know my own and my own know me." Of course the Master cares. That's the secret in handling life's storms. Life can be tough at times. Disease, danger, and death are all part of life. But God is greater and God's love is infinitely more secure.

"My sheep hear my voice. I know them and they follow me." Hearing is believing and believing is following. Hearing the voice of Jesus means trusting that God is greater. It means listening to Jesus and following him.

Missionary Herb Schaefer tells about a thirteen-year-old Chinese girl who continued with her family to worship God secretly in their home during the Cultural Revolution in China, that time when religion was forbidden and worship was banned by the Chinese rulers. One evening the Red Guards burst into their small home and threatened them for worshiping Jesus. A small altar with a crude cross stood in one corner of the room. Determined to put a stop to their worship and command complete allegiance to the Communist state, the Red Guard lieutenant demanded they spit on the cross. They refused. The lieutenant became indignant and shouted at them that unless they spat on the cross they would be killed.

Finally the elder in the group came forward, spat on the cross and left. One by one they followed, doing the same disgusting thing until only the thirteen-year-old remained. She refused to do what the others had done. "I cannot and I will not," she replied. Then she told the lieutenant the depth of her faith and said that she was willing to die for it. Remarkably the Lieutenant seemed pleased. "This is the kind of devotion we want for the new China: people who will commit themselves so totally that they are willing to die for what they believe." But he wanted that devotion directed toward Chairman Mao. "We will change you," he promised and left. She was spared, but she never saw the rest of her family again.

The story doesn't end there, however. For shortly thereafter, that little girl fled to Hong Kong and was taken in there. Later she entered the Lutheran seminary there and today she is a pastor of the Hong Kong Lutheran Church, serving the needs of countless souls. She prays for the day when she will be allowed to return to her village and minister to her people there and perhaps even to that Red Guard lieutenant who spared her but murdered her family.

She was able to endure, to overcome that tragedy in her life, because she knew the Good Shepherd. She had heard God's voice and she knew that God is greater. God is greater and our devotion to God can give us strength to endure as well. We may not be able to still the storms of life that rage around outside us. But with a strong Captain at the helm of our ship, with a Shepherd to lead us, his voice to heed and follow, we can calm the storms within us. For it is not what happens *to* us that matters as much as what happens *in* us. That's why Jesus says to us today, "I know my own and my own know me. The sheep hear my voice and follow me." In the midst of the storms of life, let us listen to the gentle voice of Jesus saying, "Peace. Be still." For God is greater. In Jesus' name. Amen.

Strike Up
The Band

A junior high music teacher had just organized a band in her school. The principal was so proud of the music teacher's efforts that without consulting her he decided that the band should give a concert for the entire school. The music teacher wasn't so sure her young musicians were ready to give a concert, so she tried to talk the principal out of holding the concert, to no avail. Just before the concert was ready to begin, as the music teacher stood on the podium, she leaned forward and whispered to her nervous musicians, "If you're not sure of your part, just pretend to play." And with that, she stepped back, lifted her baton and with a great flourish brought it down. Lo and behold, nothing happened! The band brought forth a resounding silence.

Sometimes we in the church are like that junior high band, unsure of our parts, tentative in our roles, reluctant to trumpet forth the music of faith that God desires of us. And that's because we have trouble deciding what's most important to us.

An incident a couple of summers ago in San Antonio, Texas, illustrates what I'm talking about. It was a hot, 99-degree August day when a ten-month-old baby girl was accidentally locked in a parked car by her aunt. Frantically the mother and the aunt ran around the auto in near hysteria, while a neighbor attempted to unlock the car with a clothes hanger. The infant was bawling at the top of its lungs, beginning to turn purple and foam from the mouth, a combination of anxiety and the intense heat inside the car.

It had quickly become a life-and-death situation when Fred Arriola, a tow-truck driver, arrived on the scene. He grabbed a hammer from his truck and smashed the back side window of the car to free the baby. Was he heralded a hero? Not so. According to an article in the San Antonio *Tribune*, he is quoted as saying, "The lady was mad at me because I broke the window. I just thought, 'What's more important — a baby or a window?' "

Most of the choices we make in life are not between what is trivial and what is important. Rather, most of the choices we make are usually between what is important and what is more important. This morning's Gospel reading is so timely for us because it shows us what is most important.

As we gather in worship today we affirm that the greatest blessing that God has given us is God's love for us — God's love that forgives us our sins and makes us children of God; God's love that brings us together into a fellowship with one another; God's love that sends us forth to proclaim the death and resurrection of Jesus, our Savior. As God's people we gather together in this congregation to affirm to one another what is most important for us — God's love.

As Jesus says this morning, "A new commandment I give to you: that you should love one another, even as I have loved you, you should love one another. By this all will know that you are my disciples, if you love one another."

Note, dear friends, that most of all, first and foremost, that which God desires of us is that we love one another. We may tithe. We may teach. We may sing or serve or sacrifice. We may visit on behalf of our congregation, preach the Gospel, clean the kitchen, sew the quilts, sponsor the youth, mow the grass. And all of these things are of vital importance to a congregation. They are wonderful and important to our life together. But if we do not do them out of love for God, if we do not love one another, we miss what God desires most of us.

Lucy stands with her arms folded and a resolute expression on her face, while Charlie Brown pleads with her. "Lucy," he says, "you must be more loving. The world needs love. Make this world a better place, Lucy, by loving someone else." At that Lucy whirls around angrily and Charlie goes flipping over backwards. "Look, you blockhead," Lucy screams. "The world I love. It's people I can't stand!"

And I think that sometimes we can identify with that remark. It's easy to love in the abstract — the world, people in general. We have no problem with that. It's people around us that drive us crazy. And yet it is precisely those people around us, people nearest to us, with whom we work and go to school, neighbors next door, and the people we sit next to in church, that Jesus calls us to love.

Love in action — that's what we are talking about this morning. Love which finds expression in kindness, courtesy, tolerance, and acceptance of those around us. Jesus calls us to love one another and to bring that love to light in the way that we treat those around us. It's easy to love people in general, to affirm that love is a good thing and something we all need. But it's another thing altogether to put that love into action, to make love concrete in our attitudes and actions toward others. Someone once said, "We are judged by our actions, not our intentions. We may have a heart of gold, but then, so does a hard-boiled egg."

Love one another. As a congregation of God's people, we are called to care for one another, to set aside our preconceived notions of who is and who is not acceptable to God. For the ground at the foot of the cross is level. We are all sinners. We have all fallen short of the glory that God expects of us and we are all received into God's goodness by God's grace, not by our own doing. It is God's love that unites us and it is God's love that we are called to share with each other.

That means that our lives must be characterized by love in action. Jesus says, "As I have loved you, love one another." Take all the psychology texts written and boil them down to their essential truth and you'd have difficulty coming up with a better rule for life than that. "As I have loved you, love one another." Most authorities tell us that love is a learned response. Just as the abused often becomes an abuser, so the one who is loved learns to love.

That's what we are talking about this morning: learning to love one another. Our Christian congregation has the purpose to model love for one another and in doing so to help us learn to love. Look at the foundation of this love laid for us. *(Here the preacher may wish to include a brief history of the congregation and its pastors, lay leaders and those significant to its life.)* We affirm that God has laid a good foundation for us. And in the center of this foundation is Jesus Christ. We might well say with Saint Paul, "I have resolved to know nothing among you except Jesus Christ and him crucified." The source of our love and of our blessing is Christ Jesus.

So we know that the word that Jesus gives us today, this command to love, is not a legalistic requirement laid upon us by Jesus. Rather it is the natural response of our hearts to the love that we have received from God through Jesus. The love given to us is the unconditional, undeserved, unlimited love of Christ for us — an example of love in action.

Jesus says, "As I have loved you, love one another." The truth is that we love because he first loved us. We enjoy the benefits of this congregation because others experienced God's love and decided to share that love with others. They experienced God's love for them and sacrificed and shared to make God's love the foundation of this congregation. And now it is our turn. It is our time to experience God's love and share it with others. It is our turn to experience God's love in action in our lives and to sacrifice to make it real for others.

We live in a world that is increasingly hostile to the Christian faith, a world that grows more and more self-centered every day, a world that has lost the meaning of the word "sacrifice," that does not understand the commitment of faith. This is the world in which we are called to share God's love, but we also admit that we are part of this world. We are among those who find it difficult to love others. We are among those whose time is limited and who find it difficult to make time for the church. We are among those who often fail to share God's love with others, whose offerings for the church are often far from "sacrificial."

As we gather today and hear Jesus' word to us, our prayer is that God would strengthen us for service to God and help us to love one another. We pray that God would use the example of Jesus' love in action to teach us how to love as well, to show us how to give of ourselves for others, and to lift our vision to heaven above and set us afire with faith. Love for one another is the primary witness of the church in the world today. Jesus made that clear when he said, "By this shall all know that you are my disciples, if you have love for one another."

A number of years ago Henry Drummond wrote a classic sermon titled "The Greatest Thing in the World." He concluded his sermon by suggesting that if you put a piece of iron in the presence of an electrified field, that piece of iron itself will become electrified. And in the presence of that electrical field, it is changed into a magnet. As long as it remains in contact with that field of power, it will continue to attract other pieces to itself. We are like that piece of iron. In the presence of Christ, we experience his love and take on his likeness. We are changed, electrified by the Holy Spirit, to attract others to the same love of God that we experience.

Our Christian discipleship, living as faithful members of the church, is not just a matter of willpower. It is not just deciding that we will do it, that we will love others. It just doesn't happen that way. It happens far more simply than that. Sharing God's love, living God's love, loving one another happen when we are connected to God's love, when we allow God's love to sur-round us, to shape and mold our lives in Jesus' image. In a world all too often filled with people concerned about themselves first, characterized with an impersonal "what's in it for me" attitude, we are called to witness to something more important — love that gives of itself for others; love that cares about others; love that makes our lives meaningful and significant in giving to others.

So take up your instruments and play! Let the band of faithful strike up a tune, for the musical score, the notes, are laid out before us. Jesus says, "As I have loved you, love one another." Amen.

The Peace
That Jesus Gives

Easter 6   **John 14:23-29**

There is a road in southern Italy that begins in the city of Eboli and ends in the mountain village of Gagliano. To anyone who makes that journey, it is an ascent to hell. Gagliano is no more than a scattered cluster of fallen down whitewashed old buildings, hanging desperately to barren slopes near a rocky cliff. The village has been there for centuries and for as far back as the oldest person can remember, it has always been a place of severe poverty, unrelenting disease, frightening superstition, monotonous despair, and death. Oppressed and defeated by those conditions, it is said that the peasants of Gagliano do not sing and there is a saying among them that "Christ stopped in Eboli," that somehow God had forgotten them and Christ stopped at the other end of the road. Because hope and joy, the fullness of human life that God means for us to have, are not found there, the road to Gagliano is a road that leads to hell.

Likewise, there are some stairs in a New York City tenement that go up six flights to an apartment that houses a family of ten — a grandmother, her two daughters and their seven children. Anyone who has climbed those stairs and shared in the experiences of that family this past year has made an ascent to hell. Unemployed, with few or no job skills, the family subsists on welfare payments and the meager wages one daughter brings home from work at a fast-food restaurant. Often the heat does not work and there is no hot water. Many days there is no food, for alcohol and drugs often eat up their money. Five days before Christmas, while the grandmother was down on the first floor to fetch the mail, one of the little boys climbed up on the gas stove, turned it on and set himself ablaze. While the rest of the world was singing "Joy to the World," that family, already dead to the world around them, mourned the painful death of one of their children.

In another part of the world, there is a trail in eastern Turkey that winds its way through the rocky barrens to the squalor of a refugee camp. Here thousands of people are housed in makeshift tents — tattered blanket homes. If you were to take that road and visit those camps, you would hike yourself into hell. Sickness and disease are rampant there. Death is a frequent visitor where fresh water and food are scarce and sanitary conditions are unheard of. The people who live in those camps are trapped — unable to move forward into Turkey and, because of war and fighting behind, unable to go back to their homes.

In this so-called modern world, which is supposed to be undergoing a revolution of change in the direction of a "new world order," so many of its roads lead not up, or forward, into the future, but back and down into hell. Death travels these roads in Ryder trucks, driven by paranoid patriots, loaded with fertilizer explosives. Sickness stalks the streets of Zaire under the name of the Ebola virus. In fact, all over our world there are streets and stairways, elevators and superhighways that lead to hell, places of evil where people are trapped in boredom, bigotry, loneliness, leukemia, poverty, psychosis, despair, and death.

Trouble is all about us and the words of Saint Paul ring true when he wrote, "Outwardly we are wasting away. Daily we are being given over to death." To us Jesus speaks this morning, saying, "Peace I leave with you. My peace I give to you. Not as the world gives do I give to you. Let not your hearts be troubled. Neither let them be afraid."

Jesus was preparing his disciples for tough times. He was about to ascend to the Father and they would be on their own — left to find their way through this world alone. And yet, they would not be alone. For he would be with them in the presence of the Comforter, the Counselor, the Holy Spirit. In 1520 Ferdinand Magellan battled for an entire year to find a passage around South America. There at the very tip of the continent, in its icy waters he encountered some of the worst weather anywhere on earth. Raging seas, towering ice floes, and a mutinous crew plagued his efforts. When he finally made his way through those straits (which today bear his name — the Straits of Magellan), he entered into a great body of water that lay beyond, and as he and his men lifted their faces to heaven and gave thanks to God, he named the new ocean "The Peaceful One — the Pacific Ocean."

In his words this morning, Jesus desires to lead us in the same way to a place of peace. It is his hope to direct our feet and steer our lives from the paths that would lead to hell to his place of peace. "Let not your hearts be troubled," he says, "neither let them be afraid."

Those are important words because our world is filled with fearful people. Advice columnist Ann Landers receives something like 10,000 letters a month. When asked what seems to be the most common topic, she answered that most people seem to be afraid of something. They are afraid of losing their health, their job, or their family. They are afraid of upsetting their neighbor, alienating a friend, or committing a social faux pas. Many are even afraid when there is no reason to be afraid. Ours is a world of fearful people.

Psychologist Hugh Missildine says that among the earliest emotions that every human being experiences as an infant is the feeling of fear. And that fear can be grouped into three distinct categories: a fear of falling, a fear of loud noises, and a fear of abandonment. As we grow into adults, we are able to deal fairly well with two of those fears. For some, of course, the fear of heights still remains and even though as we grow old we regain that fear of falling and breaking a bone, it is not the same as the fear of falling that a baby experiences. Likewise as we grow older, we lose our fear of loud noises, even though many a parent has experienced it just the same — this time, however, it's rock music coming from a teenager's room.

Most people learn to deal with those two fears. But the fear of abandonment, of being left alone, of having no one who cares about us, is a fear that all people share, and for many it just grows more acute the longer we live. To us Jesus says this morning, "That can't happen. I will never leave you alone. I am going to my Father, but I will send the Holy Spirit to be with you."

Every basketball fan knows the name Larry Bird. An All-Star player for the Boston Celtics for many years, Larry Bird won nearly every award a basketball player can win. And yet he still remembers what it was like to be overlooked and unappreciated. In his senior year in high school, Bird was chosen for the Kentucky/Indiana All-Star Games. Now those games are a big deal in basketball crazy Kentucky and Indiana. However, the only reason Bird was chosen was that usually there was a representative from southern Indiana and they needed someone to fill that slot. They made that clear to him when he was selected. So from the very beginning, he was placed on the second team.

In the practices, however, the second team out-played the first. And in the first game of the All-Star series, the Indiana team was up by eight points when the second team with Bird on it was sent in. They blew the game wide open. The same thing happened in the second game. This time the Indiana team was trailing in the first half when Larry's unit went in and again they went crazy and took complete control of the game. However, as the second half started, the coach put the first team back in.

Later, when it was time for the second team to go back in, the coach put everybody in except Larry Bird. He was left there, alone at the end of the bench wondering what was going on. Finally with about two minutes to play, the coach came over to Larry and said, "Hey, I forgot all about you. Why don't you go in now?" And Bird refused. "Too late, coach," he said. Years later he reflected on the event and said, "I know I overreacted because I was young. However, if I had it to do over again, I'd do the same thing because I remember how embarrassed I was. Even though my values have changed and my outlook is different, I still re-member how I felt — completely forgotten and totally unappreciated."

Friends: if one of the greatest basketball players of all time can feel forgotten, how about the rest of us who are not blessed with the talent and skill that he has? We know how it is to feel forgotten and unappreciated. We've been down that road.

But the good news this morning is that God will not forget us. God tells us that we are somebody — and in baptism God calls us by name. God puts God's mark upon us and makes us God's own. God sends us the Holy Spirit, to comfort and counsel us in life.

As Jesus called those disciples to him in the upper room and spoke the words of the Gospel reading to them, Jesus wanted them to know that they were his. He gave them a new identity and a sense of inner peace that the world could never take from them. And that's what he wants to give to us: a sense of peace, a new identity, and a direction for living so that our footsteps will not wander onto the roads to hell.

Highly esteemed author Alvin Toffler once said, "You've got to think about the big things while you are doing the small things, so that all the small things go in the right direction." And that's true. If we are to be effective and successful and happy in this life, we need to have something bigger than ourselves to strive for. Companies today urge their workers to write out a mission statement. What is our purpose in doing business? Whom do we seek to serve? How can we do it? In the same way, it would be helpful if each of us had a personal mission statement. What drives our lives? Whom do we serve? What is our purpose for living? And here's a possible answer: To live my days making my life and the lives of those around me more pleasing to God. Or: To enrich someone else's life with the love that God gives me. Or: To use my gifts, abilities, and opportunities to the utmost for God's glory. Would that kind of mission statement make a difference in how we live?

In 1991 an Air Canada flight ran into big trouble. Passengers were enjoying an in-flight movie on the Boeing 767 when the jumbo jet's massive engines abruptly stopped. At first only those without earphones on noticed anything. However, soon it was apparent the jet was in trouble. The pilot came on the speaker system and announced that Flight 143 would be making an emergency landing.

The 69 people on board were trapped in an agonizingly slow but inescapable descent to earth.

For several minutes a desperate silence hung over the cabin. Then fear gave way to screams of anxiety as the landing neared. All the latest technology could not keep the jumbo jet in the air. What had happened was this. The electronic digital fuel gauge was out of order. So the flight crew had depended on the figures given them by the refueling crew before takeoff. But someone on the refueling crew had confused pounds with kilograms. Therefore, eight hundred miles short of its destination, that mighty jet simply ran out of fuel and was forced to make an emergency landing. Fortunately no one was injured.

A multimillion dollar airplane, headed in the right direction, but running out of fuel. That's what's happening to a lot of people today. They have everything in life going for them — a new car, a wonderful home, a good education, and a good job — and one day they wake up out of fuel. At the center of their lives there is an emptiness. They don't know why they are living. There is nothing outside of themselves to live for.

Don't let that happen to you. Jesus tells us that the power for successful living comes from God. It is the promised gift that Jesus offers us. "Peace be with you," he says. "My peace I give to you, not as the world gives you. Let not your hearts be troubled, believe in God, believe also in me." In Jesus' name. Amen.

Connected
To God

The Ascension Of The Lord   **Luke 24:44-53**

In his book *On a Wild and Windy Mountain*, Dean of the Chapel at Duke University William Willimon tells of being in New Haven, Connecticut, as a student in 1970, during the famous Black Panther trial. Perhaps you remember those days — the 1970s? It was a turbulent time for our country — a time of strife, discord, and agony that threatened to tear our country apart. Much of the unrest of those days came to a focus during the trial of those Black Panther leaders. It was just at that time that Willimon happened to attend a choral mass at a Catholic church near Yale University. A boy's choir was singing a great Ascension composition called "Deus Ascendit — God Has Gone Up." As he sat there listening to those young voices, Willimon found himself thinking, "How appropriate. God has gone up. Gone up and away. God has left us to our confusion. Abandoned us in the midst of the angry shouts of the mobs, the sound of gunfire and the rhetoric of the revolutionaries." God indeed has abandoned us.

However, as he sat there and continued to listen, Willimon noticed that the boys were not singing "Deus Abscondit," which would mean "God has abandoned us," but rather they sang "Deus Ascendit," God has gone up. And the words of that song led Willimon to understand that God had not given up on us. Rather the Ascension of Jesus signaled that what Jesus had begun on earth

97

would be brought to completion in heaven even after his ascension to heaven. As we say in the Creed each week, "He ascended into heaven and is seated at the right hand of the Father." He ascended not to abandon us but to complete what he began — through the work of the Holy Spirit, through his church and through his faithful people, Christ still is at work to rule with love and mercy.

Christ has not abandoned us — but he *has ascended* into heaven and that's what the focus of our worship today is about. So important is this event that Luke describes it twice — in the last chapter of his gospel and the first chapter of Acts. The setting is the Mount of Olives. Forty days had passed since the resurrection of Jesus. It was time for him to return to heaven. And so once again, Jesus appears to the disciples. He joins them in worship. He breaks bread with them. He announces to them that they will soon receive the Holy Spirit, and when the Holy Spirit comes to them, they will be his witnesses in Jerusalem, Judea and Samaria and even to the ends of the earth. And after he has given them this assurance, he is lifted up before them into the heavens until a cloud hid him from their sight. Deus Ascendit. God has gone up.

In the first chapter of Acts, after Jesus had ascended into heaven, the disciples stood there gazing into the sky. Suddenly two men dressed in white appeared beside them and said, "Men of Galilee, why are you standing here looking up in the sky? This very Jesus who has been taken from you into heaven will come back just the same way as you have seen him go." And at this the disciples returned to Jerusalem. Upon entering the city, they went back to where they had been gathering and (Luke tells us) *"they were of one accord and devoted themselves to prayer."*

It is the first picture we have of the Church of Jesus Christ. It is the first mention of what the disciples did when Jesus was no longer with them. "They were of one accord and they devoted themselves to prayer." Imagine the effect the Ascension must have had on those disciples! They had seen Jesus physically ascend to the Father in heaven. And it was a time of joy. For they no longer had to worry about the future — for they knew that their Savior now sat at the right hand of God. They need not worry any longer because they knew they were connected to him. And because they were connected to Jesus, they felt at peace with God.

There is a humorous little story that came out of Hollywood many years ago. A famous and handsome movie star checked into a hospital. As might be expected, every nurse in the hospital was very attentive to his needs. However, one particularly attractive nurse was at his side nearly every time he moved. When he could take it no longer, he indicated that he would like to have a little time alone, and she said to him, "Sure. But remember, if you need anything at all, all you need to do is pull this cord." The movie star gave his irresistable smile and said, "Thank you, my dear, but what is the cord attached to?" She just smiled back at him and said, "Why me, of course."

The disciples knew that Jesus had ascended into heaven to be with God, the Father, and that was good news for them, because they also knew that they were connected to Jesus. And that sense of being connected to Jesus gave them confidence of faith to face the future alone. They may not have known what the future would hold for them, but they did know who held the future for them. And that was enough. That sense of being connected to Jesus enabled them to face persecution and suffering knowing that God was on their side. They could trust God because they knew Jesus.

It is said that the wife of Albert Einstein was once asked if she understood her husband's theory of relativity. She replied, "No, but I know my husband and I know that he can be trusted." The disciples knew that Jesus had ascended to be with God, the Father, and that was enough. Jesus could be trusted with their lives and hence God could be trusted with the future.

When you and I face difficulties and troubles in life, when life deals us a "bum hand" or the future looks bleak and hopeless, we need to hold on to Jesus' promise. The same Lord Jesus who welcomed the little children into his arms, the same Lord Jesus who healed the lepers and opened the eyes of the blind, the same Lord Jesus who offered himself up on the cross for our salvation now sits at the right hand of God the Father and rules over all things. He can be trusted with our days. We can depend upon him to care for us. And what a difference that can make for us. For Jesus rules over all creation and he is the head of the Church.

The disciples knew that. That's why they responded the way they did. Luke tells us that after they had returned to Jerusalem, they were all of one accord. When you think about the diverse personalities and characters who were part of that circle of disciples, that in itself is a minor miracle. The disciples' hearts were bonded together by the resurrection. It's almost as if the experience of the cross had shown them their own weaknesses — their shared failure to "buck up" and stand with Jesus in his hour of need, the betrayal of one of them, and the outright denial of Jesus by another had shown them where they all stood — each a weak, sinful human being. But more than that, Jesus' forgiveness of them, his understanding and acceptance of them and his willingness to receive them in spite of their sinfulness and his promise to use them as his witnesses had welded them together into a great unity. A unity that is a symbol of what the Church of Jesus Christ is to be.

Let me give you an example of this. When Sir Edmund Hillary and his native guide, Tensing, made their historic climb up Mount Everest, Hillary slipped, lost his footing, and fell into a treacherous crevice. Fortunately, Sir Edmund and the guide were tied together by a strong rope. The Nepalese guide, Tensing, pulled his British friend, Hillary, inch by inch back to safety. Tensing was later asked about this event and said, "Mountain climbers always help each other." There was a bond between them — figuratively and literally.

The same was true for the disciples after Jesus' ascension and the same should be true in the Church today. There is a bond that ties us together — a bond that should lead us to support one another, to reach out to each other in love — a bond that seeks to pull each other up higher and higher into God's presence.

Rebecca Manley Pippert, in her book *Out of the Salt Shaker and into the World*, gives an example of that kind of bond. She tells about a brilliant college student called Bill who became a Christian. He was part of that generation who dressed differently from their parents. For instance, he never wore shoes, no matter what the weather, and no matter where he went, he dressed in a t-shirt and jeans. In fact, even when he visited the campus church he was always dressed that way, in a t-shirt and jeans and, of course, without shoes. One Sunday during the summer, however, he decided to visit a local church near the campus. He came a little late and since the church was full, Bill walked down the aisle looking for a seat. Because of his less-than-normal attire, no one in the congregation would move in to give him a seat. So, not finding a seat, Bill sat down on the floor on the carpet in front of the front pew. You can imagine the tension in the congregation with that young man dressed in blue jeans and a t-shirt and not wearing shoes, sitting on the carpet in front of them.

Just when things seemed unbearable, an elderly man in the congregation got up from his seat and began walking up the aisle toward Bill. People looked at each other. They were certain they knew what would happen. This gentleman would ask the young fellow to get up and leave. When the older fellow came to where Bill was sitting, he stopped, and, to everyone's surprise, slowly lowered himself to the floor, and the two of them sat there and worshiped together. Naturally, at first people were shocked — but as they thought about it — they were moved. For that was an example of the kind of love and acceptance they were called to offer one another in the Church. It was an example of the bond that Jesus has forged between us through his death and resurrection.

As the Church of Jesus Christ, we are called to welcome one another, to forgive, to love, and to accept each other with the same acceptance, love, and forgiveness we have received from God. There is no room in the church for petty complaining, gossip, griping, or hurtful criticism of one another. When we cut each other up, we only destroy the bond that Jesus has died to create within us. And we end up cutting the rope that ties us to one another and to Jesus.

The disciples knew that. They returned to Jerusalem from the Mount of Olives after the Ascension of Jesus with joyful hearts, of one accord, devoted to prayer and to one another. They didn't know what awaited them. But they knew that they would need each other. Jesus had told them that they would be his witnesses in Jerusalem, Judea, and Samaria and even to the ends of the world — the same world that had arrested, beaten and persecuted him —

the same world that had tried to crucify him. It was into this same world that Jesus was sending them. And the picture that we get of those disciples is one of joy. Imagine that! They joyfully accepted Jesus' mission to take the news of his resurrection into all the world. It was a privilege for them to represent God in the world because they knew they were connected to God.

We focus this morning on the Ascension of Jesus to remind us that we also are connected to Jesus. Deus Ascendit. God has gone up! Jesus has ascended to God the Father, but not before he died for us and rose to give us eternal life. He sends us his Spirit and through Holy Baptism he makes us his church. We are those who Jesus appoints to be his witnesses. And we do that as we joyfully worship together, support one another, and serve in His name. He has not abandoned us. He has gone up and is seated at the right hand of God the Father. He sends us his Spirit to guide and direct us. And the Spirit is given to us so that we might support one another, nurture each other in faith, and work together in the unity of the Spirit. In Jesus' name. Amen.

Books In This Cycle C Series

Gospel Set
Sermons For Advent/Christmas/Epiphany
Deep Joy For A Shallow World
Richard A. Wing

Sermons For Lent/Easter
Taking The Risk Out Of Dying
Lee Griess

Sermons For Pentecost I
The Chain Of Command
Alexander H. Wales

Sermons For Pentecost II
All Stirred Up
Richard W. Patt

Sermons For Pentecost III
Good News Among The Rubble
J. Will Ormond

First Lesson Set
Sermons For Advent/Christmas/Epiphany
Where Is God In All This?
Tony Everett

Sermons For Lent/Easter
Returning To God
Douglas J. Deuel

Sermons For Pentecost I
How Long Will You Limp?
Carlyle Fielding Stewart, III

Sermons For Pentecost II
Lord, Send The Wind
James McLemore

Sermons For Pentecost III
Buying Swamp Land For God
Robert P. Hines, Jr.